REFLECTIONS
OF A
WANDERING CELT

CHRISTOPHER MAHON

First Edition June 2020 in paperback

Project by New Voices Publishing Services
guiding authors to self-publish
www.newvoices.co.za

REFLECTIONS OF A WANDERING CELT

CHRISTOPHER MAHON

CONTENTS

FOREWORD

I intended publishing this volume of poetry privately, partly for my own amusement and that of family and a few friends, but partly also, because it is impossible, as an unknown poet, to get a first volume published, for very good and obvious commercial reasons. However, a friend introduced me to the miracle of self-publishing so I thought I would give that a shot. I have always loved poetry, since being introduced to it in boarding school, and have a particular yen for the sonnets of Shakespeare, a fact which creeps into my own modest efforts, as can easily be seen, in a few of my poems. I do not claim any expertise. It would be simply foolish to do so. I am untaught, and realise a few of my poems might well be judged by some as doggerel, but I feel there are a few gems in there as well. I always think writing poetry is a bit like what laying an egg must be like – a lot of straining and pushing, and the measure of its longevity thereafter depends on the amount of warmth it receives.

In the past number of decades, most published poetry, has invariably been non-rhyming or free verse. In this genre, it appears to me, practically anything goes, once a reputation has been established, with quite a lot of what is written, seeming to be the equivalent of exhibits for the Turner prize. Most free verse seems to be "stream of consciousness" masquerading as poetry. No real effort seems to be expended, no word-smithing, no agonising, no beads of sweat on the brow, just strings of words, most of which are, literally prose, posing as poetry. Yes, there are, sometimes, beautiful thoughts there, but it is prose, and its popularity, as poetry, is a bit of mystery to me. A Thespian, Poet and Writer, called Zach Payne, recently commented that going from rhyme to free verse was a bit like taking off a corset and putting on a "T" shirt!! Robert Frost also commented that writing free verse was like playing tennis without a net! Whatever one says, the free verse genre seems to be the darling of the cognoscenti, leading to the obvious conclusion that I am living on a different planet.

Poetry must have, I feel, a degree of passion, humour, and other content, derived from the poet's own trials, tribulations, or observations. It must, on occasion, be wrung out of him, with a degree of pain and suffering, and on other occasions, "trip lightly off the tongue, as though speech were his alone", to paraphrase a line from one my own poems. It can sometimes just be amusing, or even "amusing doggerel", but ultimately it is all about taste. We are not talking here about starving in a garret for one's art, but I do feel there needs to be some evidence of effort, or struggle. This holds good for a Limerick, an Epic, a Haiku, or an Ode. Whether the poet is skilled in meter, onomatopoeia, rhyme, simile, alliteration, or just surrendering to the internal Muse, the final product must not be seen to have been thrown together after a few pints and a sharp intake of curry.

One reads that the Traditionalists want poetry to "evoke fellow feeling in others". The Modernists want "a complex web of references", and the Post-modernists want "collages of current idioms that are self-contained, and that shock, challenge, or mock pre-conceived ideas". Regardless of the Genesis, the School of Thought, or The Ethical Framework, I think that a poem has to touch people other than the poet, and not exclusively the Guardians at the Gate of 'high literature'! It should though, primarily, act as an outlet for the poet's own feelings – be a sort of cathartic valve, emitting poetic steam, and it should touch ordinary people, even if all it does, is give them a snigger or a good belly-laugh.

I tend to write a lot of Lyrical, or to the layman, rhyming poetry. A poet once commented that, "A poem without a Rhyme, is great crime"! Herman de Connick said "Poetry is the rapture of lyrical language"! I tend to agree, but this type of poetry gets a bad press. No one is writing much of it. It seems to me that modern poets are sometimes scared to write it, lest the aforementioned Guardians at the gate, strike them down for straying from the true path. It may be that the Guardians feel that there is too much craft involved, thus inhibiting the free-thinking soul. Why would a free thinker want a set of tools like some common tradesman!!

Despite what I said earlier about free verse, I decided, some years ago to write some. However, I preferred my free verse to attempt to be sonorous, fulsome, reek of the sweat of putting bricks into the hod of language, while I grunt and struggle with it, up the inclined ladder, so I could mortar it into a reasonably coherent structure. Calliope, Erato, and Euterpe were, for me, no easy task mistresses. They were channels of perspiration rather than inspiration. I found free verse could be joyful, even funny, as well as deep and reflective, and I did make an effort, yea! though I may have stumbled and fallen.

Maybe, because I am Irish, and therefore steeped in Celtic mysticism, I just like the struggle. As Oscar Wilde once said, "I was working on the proof of one of my poems all morning, and took out a comma. In the afternoon I put it back again!" Laurence Ferlinghetti commented that "Poetry is the purest of the language of the Arts. It is the tightest cage, and if you can get it to sing in that cage, it's really wonderful"! Or as Seamus Heaney once said "Poetry is an act by which the relation of words to reality is renewed"! While I seek to emulate greatness, I do not claim it, not by any stretch of the imagination.

I have taken the liberty of commenting at the beginning of each of my own poems as to why I wrote it. I realise that this may deprive future historians of endless critical opportunity in the millennia ahead (only joking)!!! but you can be the judge of that.

Enjoy, and if you don't, paper has many uses!!

Chris Mahon

June, 2020

PS

I gave a copy of my poetry to a dear friend of my youth, Marcella Camp-bell (nee Thorne) who worked in Trinity College Dublin. She showed them to Professor Brendan Kennelly, a poet of note, in April 2007, and he sent her back a letter, in longhand, a copy of which I have. It read as follows. It is the only comment by anyone of note, and an established Poet and Novelist at that, on my modest efforts.

University College Dublin Arts Building
School of English Trinity College
Dublin 2
13th April 2007

Dear Marcella Campbell,

I enjoyed Christopher Mahon's poems, especially 'Slaneyside', and 'My Garden'. These two poems are musical and detailed, full of images that are vivid, natural and convincing. I think that kind of poem, musical and pictorial, and personal, is him at his convincing best. The other po-ems such as "Conflict and Compromise" are more obviously thoughtful, even philosophical, and they say interesting and perceptive things. But I still prefer the vivid, natural poems I've already mentioned. I think Christopher Mahon should continue writing. He has a talent that is well worth developing.

With best wishes

Brendan Kennelly

Acknowledgements

My grateful thanks go to family members and to several friends who proof-read the poems and offered their unvarnished opinions of the work, all of which were relatively favourable. In particular, my sons Christopher Mahon Bsc, Actuary and Dr Connor Mahon PhD, my brother Pat in Co Mayo, and my friends Douglas McClure, Gerry Hirschon, Michael O'Brien and his wife Valerie, in Cape Town and last but by no means least Patrick O'Keefe, Lawyer and University Lecturer, New Orleans, Louisiana. I am indebted in particular to Barbara Mueller of New Voices Publishing for her patient and expert handling of the preparation of the document for publishing, and for the encouragement of my wife Margaret during the Covid 19 emergency, when I finally had the time to put a life's work into coherent shape.

ROMANCE

This poem formed part of the wedding ceremony for my second marriage.

FROM THE HEART

If I could capture sunlight, compress it in my hand,
calm a turbulent, eddying wind, make golden sea-shore sand,
encapsulate the rainbow's charm, or make life-giving air
then I could fashion your sweet form, or spin your golden hair.

If I could master music's power, distil the song of birds
assume control of an Angel's soul, spin fantasies from words,
or yet contain the gentle rain, entwine a full moon's shine,
I could recreate your graceful shape, by nature's grace designed.

If I could steal a fawn's appeal, or blood red sunset glare,
collect and comb the sea-shore foam, make joy too great to bear,
could organise all paradise, encase the grace of lace,
I could synthesise your lovely eyes, and the beauty of your face.

If I could mould the finest gold, shape stilly voids in space,
deftly form a tropical storm, make art all could embrace,
or cast a bronze to last aeons, make pristine porcelain,
then I could hold you in my arms, and know love's sweetest pain.

This one is for my present wife.

ENAMORATA

You are warm Spring evenings blessed with bird-song,
in the glow of the blazing blood-red Western sky,
drowsily dipping its grandeur in a mill-pond sea.
You are rolling froth-topped tumbling waves,
ambling airily in dream drenched foam,
billowing before the dying embers of the day.
You are the strength of spars and sails,
surfing swiftly through the blue-tinged torrent,
of a timeless turbulent tide.
You are promise in the magic of the morning mist,
seared slowly by the burgeoning sun.
You are noon-day on the grass-green ground,
sheltering shyly in a scented sapling stand,
you are mild mellow meadows in the full of day,
you are my love, what need of more to say.

This is an homage to the bard again, a sonnet, to a perceived perfection in female form. I wrote it many year's ago for my first wife, when she asked me to write something about her.

THE LOVED ONE

Where can I go your beauty to escape,
this loveliness which holds me still in thrall,
sweet symmetry and elegance of shape,
beside which other beauty tends to pall,
and not alone in form is manifest,
but deeper in the eyes, nay in the soul,
the mind which is the deeper treasure chest,
that made you from the first my only goal,
a wit and humour easy, yet replete,
with modest courage and a gentle air,
that captivates, enraptures all who meet,
this enchanting creature, radiant and so rare,
Can happiness engender such sweet pain,
appeased alone, when I see you again.

This poem chronicles the break-up of relationships, including one of my own, and the business of dealing with the aftermath.

CONFLICT AND COMPROMISE

Deep scarred, as though wounded in battle,
bright armour destroyed by the fray,
the searing incisions gouged deep in the soul,
proud defences in deep disarray,
strong battlements stormed, surrender pleas scorned,
no remedy left but to flee,
to a haven of rest, there to pray for the zest,
to shake off life's cold tyranny.

When feeling alone is lodged in the bone,
there remains but a crumbling facade,
an unruffled mien, plastered thinly on pain,
and a mind that's forever on guard.
The hurt goes down deep, a stranger to sleep,
cruelly racked by regret and remorse,
as reason recedes to permit angry deeds,
tortured logic and sometimes brute force.
Yet just under the skin, welling up to the brim,
there's the one who was lost on the way,
somewhat misunderstood, and basically good,
more bewildered with each passing day.

Time the great healer pointedly fails
to render his services free,
as insides still churn and memories burn
storm-tossed on a deep rolling sea.
Friendships are tried and many subside
leaving only a true faithful few,

who while not taking sides or widening divides,
hold a sensitive, sound, balanced view.
But their love's an aside, for it can't fill the void,
hollowed out in the harrowing fight,
between those whose love died, poisoned slowly by pride,
and fears like a child's in the night.
The threshold of pain like the winter's wild rain,
recedes and becomes less intense,
as the real world intrudes in the dark interludes,
cutting soft through the mists of pretence.
At last a dull ache, at morn when awake,
pursued by the remnants of dreams,
reminds there's no rest, from this crushing bequest,
and life slowly parts at the seams.

Now and then in this pattern of conflict
a silk thread of light can weave through,
to substitute hope for despair
with colours of delicate hue.
Unobtrusive and seldom demanding,
content but to glow in the dark,
the rare loving glance a great triumph,
or chance complimentary remark.
So often a love needing love,
its emergence a product of fate,
as though one wound were healing another,
and thus making sorrow abate.
Maybe total commitment is lacking,
on one or on both of the sides,
but a deep understanding is nurtured,
in which mutual longing abides.
The ghosts of the past may still linger,
their torture as yet unappeased,

in the birth of a burgeoning friendship,
their final defeat is perceived.

Even then, nothings finally certain.,
for doubt's a formidable brake,
as each new emotional foray,
brings a little more trust in its wake.
Tender advances and words sweetly said,
in passion or merely at play,
slowly narrow the breach and progressively teach,
a lost soul to regain the way,
until drawn from the dark and into the light,
it walks in fresh flowering fields,
in dew-bedecked corn, shining golden at dawn,
reminiscent of ancient wrongs healed.
Re-armed for the task, deftly shorn of the mask,
which long held the mind trussed in chains
the bold sally forth, exorcised of the hurt,
gripping destiny fast by the reins.
Wearing wisdom wrought of great suffering,
tempered steel from the furnace of time,
at last resolved on renewal,
and a long draught of life's heady wine.

I observed this situation in a pub. I knew the lady and gentleman concerned, and listened to the ribald comments of the other men who really did fancy themselves engaging with this lady.

UNSEEN VIRTUES

She stood adorned in beauty, object of men's desire
while her 'patient' life's companion, felt the full force of her ire,
this devoted victim, tortured soul, her twisted ego served,
in silence bore the daily bind, and stoically braved,
the rant and cant so seldom seen, by admirers of facade,
whose view from fawning vantage points are always in the shade,
denying what the heat is like, under the sun's full glare
but ready, at an eye-brow's drop, their prowess to declare.

At large these unaware opine, butter melts not in her mouth,
and 'twixt her loins imagine their personal Spring of Youth.
As if only they could really bring true happiness her way
and from her breast draw music to hold old age at bay.
Such is the weighty wisdom gained from the vantage point
of vicarious lusting lovers, whom reality disappoints,
drawn nigh the flaming fire, experience sorely earned,
the skin is peeled off wishful dreams, and reality's lesson's learned.

This poem obviously concerns itself with the effect on children of family break-up. My two seemed to weather it well, but I have seen other outcomes.

The Parting

Silence preoccupies me now
it's void an ever-present cross,
dulling and draining my reason
with its vacuity.
This bitter cup will not lightly pass,
for we once loved too much,
and in impassioned times,
begat a brace of accusations,
pointing a wagging finger at our folly.
Will they in their innocence
shrug of this crushing blow
to unprotected dreams,
despite knowing they are loved,
beyond our deep divide.
Means there were, if not the right,
to cramp our failed connubial dream,
but they, in their season, did not sin
or call unreason in
to trample on their hopes.
For now our task is clear
reduce what they can bear,
dwell not upon the wrongs
of yesteryear.

This poem is dedicated to all those who fall down and get up again, no matter the difficulties.

HOPE

No one can claim the right, to complicate your life,
or pave its precious pathways with the rough-hewn stones of strife,
but there was a deep-set sadness already planted there,
a melancholy darkness, a whispering despair,
of a maiden's dream of motherhood, of great love unfulfilled,
a yearning after happiness, a lone cry all but stilled.
It spoke of weary wasted years, of pyre-like sacrifice,
of youth and beauty vainly risked on one throw of the dice.
Yet, as the rose, whose petals close, against advancing night,
must soon unfold to boldly hold the dawn's life-giving light
your tender heart and caring soul, are meant to bloom again,
enfolded by a bright new love, secure from threat of pain,
until, at last, discarded past, like petals from a flower,
compressed in memory's pages, surrenders its dark power.

TIMELESS MIRACLE

All conquering consequence of passion,
from longing loins, in love freely given,
turbulent, tumescent interlude,
a mite cocooned in amniotic care,
long months of nervous nurturing
the swelling, stretching orb
as eager ears detect the beating heart
and hesitant hands, bestride the bustling babe.
How can you, burdened by this time-old ordeal
retain such radiant poise,
hold fast through long laborious pain,
'til a little waif against your breast is lain.
Once behold this miracle,
this wonder once address,
and glimpse in microcosm
the unlimited Universe.

This poem came together many year ago as a consequence of me knowing the daughter of an old friend, who was, to say the least, a troubled young lady, with a gift for picking wholly unsuitable men. I was very fond of her despite her eccentricities and often helped her pick up some of the pieces of her broken relationships. I lost contact with her years ago, and then suddenly ran into her in Dublin one day. Her circumstances had changed dramatically and she was now in a stable relationship.

ENCOUNTER

A welcome and timely encounter
dredged out of the shimmering past,
warm, wistful, meandering memory,
lost treasure recovered at last.
I recall a timorous schoolgirl,
in the shelter of innocent years,
full of mischievous fun and laughter,
and puberty's immature fears.
Replete even then with rich promise,
of beauty and caring and grace,
the means for the world to outwit you,
shone strong from a too-trusting face.
Our meetings, though all too infrequent,
forged strong links that quietly thrived,
through a chance meeting here or gathering there,
mellow memories renewed and revived.
Our letters exchanged, over trivia ranged,
formal, probing and often strait-laced,
could not let you hide from the need to decide
when strong feelings had to be faced.
As our loves waxed and waned,
and of mine none remained,
we were drawn to our mutual fates

'till we finally found in life's middle ground
a compromise both could embrace.
Now I can rejoice in the sound of your voice,
or the words of a letter you've penned,
and wherever the future may lead us,
I'm proud to have known you, my Friend!

LOVE AND VANITY

Too well I know my love fell short of all it was to be
I crushed its life force wantonly through the sieve of vanity
I abandoned all its promise to fulfil a grand design
to feed a proud ambition even I could not define.
I pursued a clouded chimera, that brought me nought but fear
that distanced me in space and time from all that I held dear.
Once gorged on empty treasure, the hollow vessel of success,
I see now with greater clarity, the precious jewel once possessed.
Its lustre glows more softly now, as life starts to unwind,
but yet it shines sufficiently in the caverns of the mind.
I bathe my wounded pride in its reflected light
as I contemplate its substitute, what I achieved in life,
small recompense for all the joy true love could bring instead
I look back now and rue the times that broken hearts have bled.

I wrote this poem to be included in the form of a Wedding Service for my best friend of many years Patrick O'Keefe and his lovely wife Mirna, both from the great city of New Orleans. There names form from the first letter of each line down the left hand side.

MIRNA AND PATRICK

May our love endlessly endure
Immersed in passion and desire
Rambling like a fragrant rose
Near the secret places of the heart
Anchoring deeply in the harbour of our souls
Permeating the farthest reaches of our being
Assimilating the warmth of caring commitment
Transcending turbulence and distress
Retaining a timeless tenderness
Invading ever deeper the fabric of our lives
Commanding understanding, compassion and trust
Keeping us forever one.

NATURE

As winter started to gain domination over what had been a wonderfully typical Cape Town summer, I became acutely aware of nature's unsubtle signals.

Seasons

The season is changing
I am sad
I see the migrant birds
become uneasy,
their broods reared
and ready for the road,
swirling in the azure sky
with the abandon
of joyous organised anarchy.

Soon the heavens will darken,
the leaves tan and fall
as nature falls asleep
and hibernates,
greying the world's hair
and wrinkling its brow.

We will burrow down,
embrace the change of pace,
and cling tightly
to sun-drenched dreams,
of better, bigger times,
laden with promise.

We will survive the wilt
of Winter's drawing in,

and aspire to Spring's
awakening of our
cellared aspirations,
the better for improving
with patient ageing,
as sadness fades.

I was born in Tullow, County Carlow, and two natural features dominated my life. The Blackstairs Mountains, which I could see from our garden and the Slaney River, in which, as a child, I had so much fun.

SLANEY-SIDE

When you come to seek me, come down by Slaney-side
where the valley sweeps from Knocknacree through Tullow like a tide,
where the river plunges onward, by the Blackstairs rolling ridge,
past beautiful Bunclody and on to Wexford bridge.

And when you come to seek me, down by Slaney-side
you'll likely see the Otter free, and the Badger running wild,
where Salmon leap and Trout abound, and Wildfowl gather near
as the graceful Swan and Water-hen their bustling broods still rear.

And having sought you'll find me down by Slaney-side,
patrolling on the river bank, with a Collie at my side,
among the lush green meadows, and cornfields fat with grain,
or resting down at Aghade Falls, by the Watermill's remains.

Or maybe when you seek me, down by Slaney side
you'll see me climb Mount Leinster, the heart of Carlow's pride
high in those haughty mountains, where on a clear bright day,
the view embraces all four coasts, and takes your breath away.

But most of all you'll find me, down by Slaney side,
amongst a kindly people, whose fame is justified,
for country charm and sparkling wit, and a ready helping hand,
where a stranger finds a welcome, unrivalled in the land.

Anyone who has seen the Burren in County Clare will know what I write about here. It is one of the most visited wild places in Ireland. I am told that Japanese people flock to it in large numbers every year. It has a collection of very rare species of plant.

The Burren

I stood one day at the edge of the world,
on Clare's rock-rimmed coast
with the bulk of the Burren behind me,
like nature's proudest boast
I watched the teeming sea birds
at rest on a mill pond sea,
and I searched for the Isles of Arran
which were hidden by mist from me.
The clouds hung low from the heavens
to blanket the rolling hills
and water ran fast in rivulets
over cascading granite sills
The finely focussed fanfare
of the vision before my view
filled my famished and floundering senses
with the timorous touch of dew.
And I pondered the power of Nature
to reach inside a man's soul
unscrambling the innermost feelings
of one lost and seeking a role,
in the maelstrom of life's confusion
and the terror of trying to cope,
when the spirit is striding the boards
twixt despair and developing hope.
As the sun separated the mantle
and melted the morning mist,

I straightened and sauntered with purpose
and the notion that naught was amiss,
for a banquet of flora and fauna
in a petrified landscape is laid
where the Burren abuts the Atlantic
a restorative feast lies arrayed.

A bit of whimsy that flowed from a wonderful day many years ago on Bannagh Strand in County Kerry. Seven miles of beach and the next parish is America.

TRANQUILITY

The golden sand in undulating folds
sweeps laughing, tumbling toward the rolling tide
from where the land a preening posture holds
awaiting surging sea, his eager bride.
The white-topped waves at play with sun and breeze,
are thrust upon the land with fumbling force
and stirring, swirling, foaming waters tease,
seductive suitor, sand, without remorse.
Above the Seagull's eager echo sounds
to solemnise the nuptials far below
while overall a pleasing peace abounds
untouched, unspoilt in evening's afterglow.
So far removed from taint of life's travail
the soaring Spirit wanders uncurtailed.

In my rich and varied life I have seen the topography of the wider world, lived and worked on open plains, in deserts, and in the lush savannah. Nothing gives me a spiritual lift like the majesty of the mountains in my native land.

THE MOUNTAINS

Far form the beaten path
midst the untamed mountain mass
Cromlech, Rune and Ogham stone
adorn the fern-fringed pass
guarding the languid luxury
of alluring upland lakes.
A crescendo of coruscated crags,
carry hurrying headwaters
in gravel-gritted gushing streams,
to bathe the Fir-filled fastness
teeming with forest life.
The gold-blue sun-rimmed heavens
are rent by shrieks and cries
as the sparrow-hawk swoops
and fur and feather scatter
in panic far beneath
hearts bursting in fugitive frenzy
seeking refuge from their foe.
A startled deer is frightened
by panting fretful flight
as wild goats gambol
and March hares fight,
in this hallowed hidden habitat
vouchsafed but to a few,
strayed from the ribbon highways
and foot-worn tourist traps,
in an unspoiled treasured highland
far from man's impact.

I mentioned in another poem that Mount Leinster, the third highest mountain in Ireland, was a big feature in my childhood. I once took my sainted Mother and my sister right up to the Radio Telefis Eireann mast at the top, in a car. It was a beautifully clear day and we could literally see all four coasts.

Dawn from Mount Leinster

Probing shrouding shadows in the East,
a wisp unreal, ethereal, alone,
escapes the leaden grasp, of brooding dark,
unfettering its fearsome fretting frown.
A beam of light steals softly round a cloud
and strikes the mist a gentle glancing blow,
dispersing it to myriad twinkling gems
tumbling in the half-light row on row.
Gathering strength, dewed daylight fast unfolds,
the wonder, freshness, glory of new dawn,
resplendent in a cloak of burnished gold
mischievous in delight at being born.
Then rushing forth, it clasps a world beguiled
in warm embrace, as lovers reconciled.

Who has not been inspired, sometimes awed by the splendour of a sylvan scene as Autumn claims her role in the great scheme of Nature. When I was a child we had four seasons, and, living in the countryside, we children were wonderfully attuned to the subtle changes that surrounded us in nature, knowing the name of every bird and tree.

Deciduous Trees

Deciduous trees in Autumn
are an awesome sight to me
their rich and varied colours
a joyous symphony.
The Ash, the Oak, the Willow,
the Elm and Sycamore,
vying with each other,
reds and yellows to the fore.
The Alder and the Blackthorn,
the Chestnut and the Beech,
the Silverbirch and Maple,
on the hillside out of reach,
all the feel the Winter coming,
and in that twilight hour
take time to cheer our spirits
in each russet coloured bower.
At evening in the sunset,
when early chills invade,
a challenging canvas builds and blends
in subtle sensuous shades,
'till coaxed from branch by wind and rain
cascading leaves descend,
like brightly mottled meteors,
content to meet their end,

upon the loam-soft earthen floor,
from whence their life-force came,
enduring Winter's passing pain,
until reborn again.

I was never blessed with green fingers but was persuaded by a friend many years ago to have a go. I was surprised at how much one could achieve with a little effort. The orchestral analogy did occur to me one breezy, sunny day.

My Garden

It's not the Botanical Gardens
that you can easily see
but a neat recreational retreat
from the endless extraneous melee;
the push and the pull and the pressure
of all that complicates life,
the dreary demands of commerce,
the sterile surrender to strife.
It's a pocket handkerchief refuge
protected and private and sane,
where flowers, trees, bushes and hedges,
create a refreshing refrain,
like a finely tuned favourite orchestra,
in the buzz before music begins
when the tuning of many performers
presages a hush to the din.
The Gladiolus raises his baton
leaning lightly against a backrest,
and the Climbing Roses stretch forward
as if expecting a test.
In the background, the sombre-clad Firs,
lend their immense gravitas
as Wisteria and Climbing Clematis
resemble the Woodwind and Brass.
The strings are arranged in the rockery
Azaleas, Rhododendrons ablush,
while the rumbling background percussion

is provided by each Shrub and Bush.
Of course it's just fanciful musing
as I daydream beneath the Sun's rays
luxuriating here in my garden
the source of my happiest days.

On one occasion many years ago I decided to have a go at growing some plants from seed. Some of the seeds were infinitesimally small. I was awed by the result.

Marvels

The stunning parade of marvels in our wonderful modern world
the exponential knowledge curve, science has unfurled
can create a blasé attitude, making all just commonplace
reducing virtually everything to a digital database.
How often have you hear a friend, speak in wry and wistful tones
of the "reductio ad absurdum" of life's boring monochrome,
beset by the brash and the novel, wrapped in technical parlance
longing just once to be surprised, by unscripted circumstance.
This happened to me recently, in the simplest sort of way,
when on impulse I bought a packet of seeds, to create a floral array.
Such tiny insignificant things, not too many for the price,
a substitute for potted plants, which, this time, would not suffice.
The gaily coloured packets, were peppered with puff and hype,
and I agonised for quite a while, on variety and type,
then selected two that promised accelerated growth
and a coloured cornucopia, that would rival Joseph's coat.
I planted them in potting trays and awaited the result
devotedly attending them, like the High Priest of a cult.
Within weeks a tiny marvel nudged slowly into sight
as life peeped out and edged its way shyly toward the light.
My eyes were opened wide that day, like sunlight through a door
as I realised the awesome strength of Mother Nature's power,
to so elegantly hide inside in dull and lifeless clay
such a complicated life-support, to await upon the day
when energy from sun on high and water from below,
would merge their matching magic, to allow new life to flow.
What price this age of wonders in their splenderous array
when a single simple seedling, can amaze us in this way.

THOUGHTS OF ERIN

What Irish exile's thoughts do not turn to the "old country", when abroad. My generation left in droves in the fifties because Ireland, then, was an economic backwater, priest-ridden and hide-bound. But there is something about the place, a mystic attachment that never leaves you. Ireland isn't so much a place, as an idea, a club with 5 million members, an umbilical cord that is never really cut.

THOUGHTS OF ERIN

Alas! That I should fall between two stools,
suckled as I was at Erin's rich-milk breast,
cared for by committed teachers
their love of learning, coursing through me
like a magic fog,
my stumbling intelligence informed
by the force and majesty
of our forebears greatness;
the rich banquet of the File, the Breitheamh
and the sapid Seannachaidhe,
gorging me on my country's genius,
while An Gaeilge, like mountain honey,
flowed liberally in my eager veins
the Gaeltacht and The Pale
holding uneasy truce in my confused identity.
Alas! That learning nor Eloquence
suffice in a driven world
where youth must make its Odyssey
through baffling contradictions.
The fretting soul of Fodhla
struggled in vain to hold her children
in the subtle temptations of the modern milieu,
as they strayed to the shores of the old enemy
bearing with them the love-hate bond

shackling the Anglo-Saxon and the Gael.
Those foreign familiar lands,
satisfying temporarily, material needs
but failing and failing again
to touch the questing soul
of reluctant querulous guests.
Returned from exile, primed on petty triumph
and paltry ill-remembered victories,
I am infused with Eire's beating heart
her shining new-found confidence
the surge of pride of her vibrant youth.
It was always possible.
It has happened and I'm glad.

Erin – Ireland.
Seannaichaidhe (pronounced Shannakee) – Storyteller.
An Gaeilge – The Irish language.
Gaeltacht – The Irish speaking areas of Ireland
Breitheamh – (pronounced Brehev) Judge in ancient Ireland.

John Hume, who got the Nobel Peace prize for his efforts in securing peace in Northern Ireland, was asked once on a radio programme, whether there was war on in Northern Ireland. My recollection is that he replied that if there was no war on, why did Belfast have thirteen dividing walls.

BELFAST CITY

Slow flows the Lagan, like a lazy ox-drawn wagon
meandering its way towards the sea
through a City racked with pain, branded with the mark of Cain
an open wound for all the world to see.
Those in power would have you believe, that outward signs deceive
that all is well on Shankill and the Falls,
well if this is how things are and there's no sign of a war,
why does Belfast have thirteen dividing walls.

When viewed from far away, Belfast lives a normal day,
but Police and soldiers constantly patrol
and the tension in the air, marks a level of despair
that never fails to eat into the soul.
Even taxis segregate, we shop behind security gates
in modern malls in front of City Hall,
if all is calm and so serene, in this idyllic scene
why does Belfast have thirteen dividing walls.

The tragedy is plain, both traditions are the same
scratch them both and beneath you'll find a Celt,
subtly brainwashed through the years to magnify their fears
and guarantee that hatred never melts.
The men of violence thrive, while the people just survive,
as overhead the City streets there hangs a pall,
two traditions edge to edge, separated by the wedge
of Belfast's high thirteen dividing walls.

As the Ministers of God, go about their daily job,
or tend their flocks with loving pastoral care,
do they pause each day to think, as we teeter on the brink,
of the graveyards filled to bursting point each year.
When they gaze down from the altar, or sing sweetly from the Psalter,
while believing brethren pack their churches stalls,
does each of them reflect in whichever Christian sect
that Belfast has thirteen dividing walls.

As children fill each street, always looking very neat,
in school uniforms that state which faith they claim
or play on vacant sites, ever present military might
encircles what should be a child's domain.
After all the years of gore, will we do to them once more
what has kept this lovely City long in thrall,
will we once more have to say, when the children ask one day,
Yes! Belfast needs thirteen dividing walls.

There was hope in Belfast Town when the Berlin wall came down,
that people of good will could now decide
to forge a peace at last, that would exorcise the past,
and draw back from the brink of suicide,
a people tired of strife, hungry for a better life,
'till at last through Ulster's Halls would come the call,
let the peace of Jesus reign, in our City once again,
Belfast doesn't need thirteen dividing walls.

With the coming of the Good Friday agreement Ireland entered a period of what is hoped will be lasting peace. The lovely city of Derry and its wonderful people, bore a great deal of much of the previous chaos during the Troubles.

THE COLD EARTH MOUND

"Freedom Fighter" died today at the shrine of Columcille,
once sacred Derry City, one more victim on the bill,
that mounts with every passing day, that seems to have no end,
the shooting, bombing, stoning, the City ever ringed,
by hostile staring faces, sullen looks and naked fear,
small wonder some look inward, and question why they're there.
What would Columcille have thought, the Dove of Derry's church,
could he view the daily mayhem, where once he went to search,
for peace and sweet tranquillity in the valley of the Foyle,
where blood of guilt and innocence stain daily Derry's soil.

Yet it's often futile to reflect, on things long gone and past
when the present is the torment in which the die is cast,
the die of blazing bigotry, the die of hardened views,
where neither side will yield an inch from every full church pews.
The fears of simple Godly folk, are exploited without shame
by demagogic leaders, showing no regard for pain,
their only thought is for their power, personal, complete
no sorrow in their callous hearts, as bodies fill the streets.
While they rant each day of principle, playing only for a win
their ire enables criminals on both sides to cash in,
while caught up in the middle, are those who oft have wept
their lonely lives and grieving hearts are all that they have left.
It's part of daily living, they accept it as their lot
a life long suffering people, who tomorrow, like as not,
will watch a son "die for the cause", his blood spilled on the ground
Immortalised?, nay, brutalised, beneath a cold earth mound.

The Rebel

If my long-held dream of freedom, must be snuffed out in this way,
at least I'm spared the terror of a stay at Castlereagh,
for the bullet has gone deep in me, from a British soldier's gun,
I feel the steel of death's dread grasp, blot out the rising sun.

My comrades rest my bleeding side upon our stolen car,
as thoughts of home and family come rushing from afar
will they be nearer freedom because of what I've done,
will Unionist or Englishman admit that we have won?

Or will the struggle stretch away interminably for years,
no easy resolution, while war brings bitter tears,
or will they recast history, when we have ceased to be,
will succeeding generations live their lives in harmony.

Mine never was that noble dream enshrined in Ireland's past,
bestrewn with martyred heroes and brave men unsurpassed,
I fought ingrained oppression, which faced me every day,
in streets and shops and offices, where my kind had no say.

I fought the yoke of slavery, the second rate regime,
crammed down my throat at every turn, by servants of the Queen,
and when I asked for reasons why, the reply was never vague
"so its always got to be, for every rebel Taigue."

I fought for recognition of my right to be employed,
to carry home a wage each week, to feed my wife and child,
to be accepted in my world, regardless of my views,

on politics, or Holy Writ, or paying union dues.
So while the struggle carries on into a gory dawn,
I'll be a cold statistic on a wall, when I have gone,
but one day Justice must return, to make sense of my fight,
As I lay down my burden, and embrace death's cold long night.

The 1916 Rebellion in Ireland was a magnificent event in Irish history. Few in Ireland gave the rebels a cat in hell's chance of pulling it off and they were right. However the idiotic decision by the British to shoot 16 of the leaders acted as the catalyst that turned the entire country into rebel supporters and ensured freedom. The poem is set in the epicentre of the rebellion, The General Post Office in Dublin. Far better poets have paid this tribute. This is my modest effort at doing the same.

Rebellion

Lean on your rifle in the shell-blown dust
wipe sweat from your pain-creased brow
slash-seared, blood soaked
begrimed with righteous anger.
Rest your patriotic pride
mid the ruins of apparent failure
but know this sacrifice will resonate
like a cascading carillon
in the free beating hearts
of generations of Irish yet unborn.

Your battle scarred souls
restore our nations pride
screaming daring defiance
at violent alien arrogance
a posturing power brought low
by little more than an improbable idea
unearthed from the greatness
of ancient Celtic sacrifice
so long subdued, now given new life
by unlikely defeated Heroes.

This poem started off as an attempt to explain the complexities of a divided Ireland, and the reason for the troubles, to British people, who had no idea, how or why it all came about, much less how it would all end.

THE ENGLISH TROUBLES

What would Mother England do if the winds of change that blew
caused Albion to suffer Ireland's fate
Say World War Two was won, not by Britain, but the Hun,
and four hundred years had passed since that sad date.

Let's say Hitler gained the prize and to everyone's surprise
conquered England, Wales and Scotland as he'd planned.
Then because the Reich was skint, he paid the Wehrmacht for
their stint,
with the six south western counties of the land.

For the next four hundred years, these German Planters had no fears,
as they enjoyed the power and influence of Berlin,
whilst stout English hearts of oak, suffered long beneath the yoke
of Jackboot Justice practised on their kin.

Hans played cricket on the green, and was very often seen
dancing round the Maypole like a loon.
He swapped Lager for Pale Ale, and in Autumn slaughtered quail,
but still goose-stepped at the Schutzenfest in June.

Four centuries then passed, and Britons freed themselves at last
from the darkness of the long Teutonic night
but the bitterest pill of all, over victory cast a pall
six south western counties stayed within the Reich.

Within this mini German land, a minority British band
of patriots want the Union Jack unfurled,
while suffering the sad plight of having no minority rights
just like others of their ilk, throughout the world

But German planters could now claim, since now English in the main,
Mother Deutschland claimed their loyalty of late,
"No Surrender" their proud cry, on the Reich we will rely,
"What we have, we hold, within our little State!"

Who could blame the Natives when they say, we have formed
the "BRA"
to eradicate the yoke of German might.
With the ballot box and gun, we'll overcome the dreaded Hun
replacing German gloom with Saxon light.

The BRA prove very good, and after years have long withstood,
all that Deutschland's forces threw into the mix.
No matter how hard the loyalists tried, they could not stem the tide
of the BRAs bustling bag of endless tricks.

Tanks, Guns, Reichmarks then pour in, to shore up this bottomless
bin,
until finally, the weary Chancellor calls a halt,
"We'll pull out and save some pride and not a little of our hide,
without admitting that this mess was all our fault.

Is this too fanciful or unreal, or does it really have the feel
of what happened in Ireland in its day,
would it have the same effect, if you pause just to reflect,
In Great Britain, had Hitler won the day.

Anyone who has had the opportunity to visit the National Stud in Kildare will know what I am attempting here. The Irish horse is famed throughout the world. Even the Arabs, who bred the stallions from which every racehorse to-day is descended, have studs in Ireland.

THE IRISH HORSE

Sinewy splendour, bravest breed,
packed with pulsating power
proud, haughty, full of fire,
bridled by man's brutality,
and over-arching need and greed,
presented at a melange of musters
for the awed admiration of the throng.
Seldom has pedigree
been welded into such breathless beauty,
as in the high-stepping blood-lines
of the incomparable Irish horse.
From time of the ancients
Eireann's lime rich greenness
nurtured sinew and bone
fashioning wild wind swiftness
and graceful gait,
drawing wide-eyed worshippers
of winged Pegasus of the north,
in journeying multitudes
to kneel at an equine shrine
on the broad acres of Eire.
Noble you are and fleet of foot
stunning to behold
in the controlled volcano
of your muscled majesty.

You enrich our world,
with the majestic edifice
of your puissant power,
your thunderous prowess.

Ireland is blessed with a rich literature and folklore. Many of its epic tales involving the Fianna and the Red Branch Knights of Ulster are up there with the literature of Rome and Greece. The Tain Bo Cuailgne, Bodach an Cota Lachtna, Toraioch Diarmaid agus Grainne, were often read to my generation of children in primary schools in Ireland and were the equivalent of Television series to-day. We couldn't wait for the next episode to be read, so exciting and fabulous were the tales. This is my modest effort to put into poetry one of the great love stories of all time.

TORAIOCHT DIARMAID AGUS GRAINNE

The Pursuit of Diarmaid and Grainne

Fionn, great leader of the Irish host,
leant heavily upon his burnished shield,
sweat glistened on his face,as he sat
to rest upon a hillock nigh the field,

drinking deeply from the wine-gorged horn
dangling loosely from his circling crios   (crios – a belt)
with weary sigh, he laid his war spear down
and stared upon the sky to reminisce.

Bran and Sceolaing, his faithful hunting hounds
ever by the noble Chieftain's side
rested neat their master on the ground
their loyalty to the warrior true and tried.

Towering giant, muscled to the core,
and still a potent force despite the years
that wore deep valleyed furrows in his brow,
lining his golden hair and grizzled beard.

Below him battle trained, the Fianna stood
their will and strength and military prowess,
the guarantee of Ireland's nationhood
their loyalty to Fionn, there to profess.

Each warrior to be certain of his place
beneath a branch, no higher than his knee
must run and never loose a single pace
then clear a face-high branch upon a tree.

Armed only then with wand of hardened wood
and buried to the waist within a mound
defend himself against a shower of spears
emerging from this test without a wound.

Then must negotiate the forest at great speed
and pluck a thorn from under his bare sole
breaking not a twig as he proceed,
with loss of not a single hair, his goal.

Twelve books of poetry must he now recite
no line of these to be repeated twice
and finally must, when his troth he plight
take no dowry when he choose a wife.

The hosting ended, Fionn bid his Captains dine
Oisin, Diarmaid, Oscar, Cailte, Conan too
to help him quaff a brimming skin of wine
and while away the evening's afterglow.

He spoke of his great loneliness in life,
Manissa his late wife now long deceased,
he missed her tender ways, and wise advice,
her presence at each host and kingly feast.

Oisin, devoted son of Fionn's first wife,
felt keenly in his heart, his father's pain
and urged that Fionn no longer be alone
but seek another wife and wed again.

Then rose Dering and to his Chieftain said
Cormac, our High King, lies ever in your debt
and will not see you with an empty bed
when his fair daughter Grainne is unwed.

She is the greatest beauty in the land
skilled in every woman's craft and wile
it's said she sings as sweetly as a bird
her voice the God's could easily beguile.

Her hair is golden as the rising sun
her eyes as blue as any peaceful sea
her mind is sharp, and full of gaiety
matched only by her calm serenity.

Her eyebrows a pen-stroke upon a chart
her lips as soft and red as any rose
her voice a sweet love tune to any heart,
lucky the man to whom, she, her heart bestows.

The counsel of his Captains being strong
Fionn bade Oisin mount his swiftest steed
and seek the lovely maidens hand 'ere long,
King, Cormac, tell at once his pressing need.

Wind-swift he rode and came to Tara's mound
great seat of Eireann's High and noble King
whose Halls and Houses occupied the ground
as far as eye could see, on every wing.

Before the puissant monarch came he then
and plead his case for Grainne's unwed hand
but Cormac would not straight-way lightly bend
to satisfy his Champion's strong demand.

The Princess upon hearing the debate
asked of her father who had sought the boon
and learning Fionn Mac Cumhaill would be her fate
agreed the Fianna's Chief could be her groom.

So great a warrior, noted for his deeds
of great estate and princely noble birth
her wishes for a husband would exceed
the best of men alive upon the earth.

And so a wedding feast was put in train
the noble families all to Tara came
to honour Fionn and Grainne's noble name,
and Clann Mac Airt, of ancient Celtic fame.

Upon Fionn's breast a shining golden Torc
gifted for the wedding by the King
whilst Grainne wore a long bejewelled cloak
with diamonds woven, and with pearls strung.

Her skirt of finest shining silk was spun,
held to her slender waist by golden crios
her coronet of gold outshone the sun
her visage set with look of deepest bliss.

The bride outshone each noble lady there
from jewelled shoe to golden shining hair
no woman in the land could yet compare
with this sweet maiden, graceful and so fair.

Fionn gazed with awe and wonder at her face
so delicate, alluring, yet so strong,
this feminine Princess of the Celtic race
captivating the august assembled throng.

Munster, Leinster, Connaught, Ulster too
in proud array took precedence in the room
their fealty to their High King to renew
and show respect to royal bride and groom.

The feast began with tables laden down
with gold and jewelled gifts from Eireann's clans
the bards recited tales of great renown,
of battles with the Tuatha de Danaan.

The harpists, singers, acrobats and clowns
made merry as the wine flowed like a stream
and every noble made his thirst to drown
as Prince and Warrior revelled in the scene.

One Warrior alone caught Grainne's gaze
as he sat twixt Oisin brave and Conan Maol
a handsome youth to set a heart ablaze
no more fine example of a manly Gael.

Diarmaid O Duibhne, who sat with Oisin's son,
was close companion of the Fianna Chief
accompanied him on every battle run
and shared with him his triumphs and his grief.

Upon Diarmaid's forehead was a magic mole
that seen by any woman made her fall
surrendering her body and her soul
to end, despite her herself, in total thrall.

The Fianna knowing this was so
made Diarmaid wear a band upon his head
for as sure as Diarmaid had the mole on show
an avalanche of maiden's tears were shed.

Alas! The wine had flowed that day too well
and Diarmaid's headband slipped a mite aside
Grainne saw and nothing then could quell
her love for Diarmaid burning deep inside.

She summoned her handmaiden to her then
and bade her fill a goblet to its lip,
then secretly poured a potion in
and bade her ask each warrior take a sip,

save only Diarmaid, who should not parktake,
as this was not conducive to her scheme
the wedding feast with Diarmaid to forsake
and flee with him pursuing love's sweet dream.

The Guests all drank and slumber claimed them all
as Grainne crossed the room to Diarmaid's side,
to plead that they escape before nightfall
and use this time to find a place to hide

from the anger of her father and her groom
who would pursue them to the bitter end
to seek revenge upon them all too soon
the slight upon their honour to defend.

At first the noble warrior plead his case
that honour forbade him to agree
to betray and take Fionn's proper rightful place
and with his bride elope and seek to flee.

Then angered Grainne placed on him a geas (geas-a sacred obligation)
so powerful he could not refuse her plea
but must if Celtic custom claim its place
obey the maiden's wishes to be free.

So overpowering were her dire demands
realising he would not escape some blame
two swift horses to his chariot now he spanned
and fled with Grainne swiflty oer the plain.

Many leagues they journeyed at great speed
until the mighty Shannon river hove in sight
then knowing that the chariot tracks would lead
the Fianna trackers to his line of flight

he took the fearful Grainne in his arms
and holding her above the river flow
walked in the stream the trackers to disarm
then laid her down upon a high plateau.

Then did Diarmaid make a handsome hut
of saplings gathered from the forest there
seven magic doors in it he put
lest Fionn's great host catch them unaware.

Back at the feast Oisin was first to rise
and knew at once what both his friends had done
as the King and Fionn, awoke to the surprise
that bride and Diarmaid from the feast had flown.

Great anger at this treachery filled Fionn's heart
the slight upon his honour and his name,
he thereupon swore a mighty oath
for vengeance to assuage this mighty pain.

The sons of Neachtain sent he then forthwith
to track the fugitives to their lover's lair,
and wait upon his arrival with
the Fianna Army, to apprehend the pair.

Clann Neachtain did not need all of their skill
the chariot tracks to follow to the end
by the mighty rolling Shannon's torrent 'til
no further sign was seen of foe or friend.

When Fionn arrived there with the Fianna host
the sons of Neachtain knew not where to turn
Fionn threatened then to hang them from a post
unless they found whereto the pair had run.

The trackers in the torrent forthwith dived
and downstream came soon upon the scene
where Diarmaid and his lover had emerged
and found their hut part hidden by a screen

of fresh cut branches hewn from the trees
to camouflage their presence from the world
at their love nest wherein to take their ease
and hide from their pursuers undisturbed.

The lovers quickly sealed their love-nest's doors
and barred them strongly from the room within,
as hordes of Fianna warriors threatened war
to assuage the insult to their leader Fionn.

Diarmaid knew right then, there was no chance
to flee from such a mighty horde of men
and sought to contact through a magic trance
his foster father Aonghus by the Boyne.

Descended from the Tuatha de Danaan
in magic skilled, the ancient Irish race
at Moytura field against the Celts were drawn
and lost in Eire ever more their place.

Aonghus the Danaan, sensing Diarmaid's need
put round his body a Druidic magic cloak
and in a tryst was by his foster's side
to offer his protection at a stroke.

Let me place my cloak around you both
I can whisk you with my magic to my lair
safe from Fionn and the Fianna's angry host
no more a prey to worry or to care.

But Diarmaid could not agree this plan
bidding Aonghus take Grainne right away
to leave him deal alone with angry Fionn
or escape and lead the Fianna host astray.

I cannot leave "mo gra-geal" all alone   (mo gra-geal – my bright love)
spoke up the maiden strongly, wreathed in tears
to face the awesome danger when I'm gone
leaving me to worry and my fears.

Diarmaid would have it no other way
and Aonghus wrapped her closely in his arm,
to wrap the magic cloak around her waist
and speak the magic words of the Dannaan.

His love now safe, beyond the Fianna's wrath
the first of seven doors now Diarmaid chose
demanding who outside still blocked his path,
'till Caoilte mac Ronan, first arose.

He swore to protect him from Fionn's ire
but Diarmaid could not let Ronan take the blame
and moved to ask who blocked the second door
Conan and Clann Morna's answer came.

Come out and no harm will come to you
cried Conan who stood there with his clan
that Fionn would kill the warrior Diarmaid knew
and chose the third door to proceed his plan

there Goan of the Fianna loudly claimed
under my protection will you stand this day
as Diarmaid the fourth door swiftly gained
where the Ulster Fianna waited for the prey.

McGloir of Ulster and his noble clan
friends of Diarmaid since he was a lad
he could not make sworn enemies of Fionn
so turned him to the fifth house door instead.

Oisin, Dering, Oscar stood without
but could not convince their friend to leave his lair
Diarmaid chose the sixt door with a shout
As his enemies Clann Neamhain, waited there.

We will slay you once you exit shouted they
but Diramaid held this mob in deep contempt
he had defeated them in many an affray
he would escape or die in the attempt.

The seventh door the Leinster Fianna held
and Fionn stood stoutly with them as their Lord
armed with spears, in battle they excelled,
as Fionn stood glowering with a drawn sword.

The door burst open, Diramaid fully armed
with hefted lances held in either hand
then planting them firmly in the ground
he vaulted o'er their heads with one great bound.

He ran as fast any any winter wind
to the Wood of the Two Swallows on a hill
where Grainne and Aonghus a boar had skinned
and he could now sit down and eat his fill.

He could now with his love abide
although guilt of his betrayal was not small
that night they slept together side by side
and knew the bliss of love that conquers all.

On the morrow Aonghus watched as they both ate
and witnessed love he'd never seen before
he knew such love was hard to emulate
a love that emanated from their very core.

Yet Aonghus knew his hideout by the Boyne
lay too near Tara and might just Fionn alert
he would not let up looking for their sign
they must forthwith flee into the West.

But first he warned they should never cook
or in the same place eat their daily food
and when they sleep upon some shady nook
be sure to move unto another wood.

They fled then swiftly heading further West
and found a refuge by a rushing stream
Diarmaid caught a salmon for their feast
then held his love beneath a full moon's beam.

Further West they fled until the noon
and found a resting place within a glade
where to them came a warrior called Muadhan
sent by Aonghus to guard them where they lay.

He carried them 'cross rivers deep in spate
and found for them a safe place in a cave.
He fished and cooked and guarded at the gate
and moved again the danger being grave.

Next day Diarmaid went hunting far for game
Muadhan slept from guarding 'gainst the foe
when from a hill above the rolling main
Diarmaid saw three ships, upon the sea below.

Three men well armed, caparisoned for the fray,
climbed the hill where Diarmaid stood in wait.
when asked their business for the coming day
they were happy their story to relate.

Three Kings from Scotland are we to Eireann called
to track the traitor O'Duibhne and his bride
Fionn of the Fianna promised Irish gold
If we track this lowly traitor to his hide.

Three great blood-hounds to this place we brought
who never fail to bring their man to ground.
they asked Diarmaid if he had seen the man they sought
and Diarmaid said he saw him Eastward bound.

Immediately to the cave O'Duibhne raced
Grainne and Muadhan to alert
whereupon they ran much further to the West
as the lovers tired, Muadhan carried them aloft.

Realising how all three had been deceived
The Kings with hounds returned and set them loose
and soon the fugitives scent the hounds perceived
at speed they sought to slowly close the noose.

The first was killed by Muadhan's small pet dog
the second one despatched by Diarmaid's spear
the third one's brains dashed out upon a rock
by Diarmaid as it leapt into the air.

Then followed all three Kings now fully armed
as Diarmaid launched his spears into their hearts
leaving them to rot, and still unharmed
the lovers then made ready to depart.

To the Forest of Dubhrus came the runaways
where Muadhan bade a short and sad adieu
as Aonghus only granted him three days
his time as guardian with them now was through.

Diarmaid made a refuge for his wife
and hunted in the forest for their food
being careful not to cause any noise or strife
he kept the peace as strongly as he could.

Searbhan, the Giant Guardian of the Forest
known to be bad-tempered and alone
the Guardian of the magic Quicken tree
ensured no berry from the magic tree was torn.

For each berry held the power of longer life
and freedom from sickness evermore
if eaten by mortal man or wife
they would never die in time of peace or in war.

No weapon could the Giant Searbhan wound
no fiery brand with which he could be burned
nor water course in which he could be drowned
but with three blows from his own club could be downed.

At the Hill of Allen fretted Fionn Mac Cumhaill
when two young warriors braved his centre court
sons of the McMorna clan knelt at his foot-stool
and begged the Chief their great plan to support.

You are the sons of Andala and of Art
who slew my father on Cnucha's field
I banished you, their sons, to live apart
I have not ever had that law repealed.

They begged of Fionn a pardon to receive
and in the Fianna retake their father's place
in anger Fionn offered a reprieve
for the head of O'Duibhne in a vase.

Then Fionn Mac Cumhaill made one last request
five berries from the Quicken tree to bring
but Oisin advised they abandon this sad quest
saying they'd lose their heads attempting this mad thing.

Their desire to rejoin the Fianna uppermost
they set their sights upon the dangerous chore
they travelled 'till they came near Diarmaid's post
and came upon him standing by his door.

Fionn has bade us kill you now they said
or bring some berries from the Quicken tree
but since the Giant makes the tree his bed
killing you is what will set us free.

Within a trice Diarmaid had them trussed
and lying in a heap upon the earth
about to despatch them with sword thrust
as Grainne pleaded softly they be spared.

I long for berries from the tree she cried
and three of you will see the Giant dead
appealing then to Diarmaid's warrior pride
she forced the three to seek the Giant's head.

The Giant barred the Quicken tree from them
as Diarmaid asked to pick the dangling fruit
you shall not partake the Giant said to them
as Diarmaid stood before the giant brute.

With his great club the Giant rained three blows
that shattered Diarnaid's shield above the brace
as he slid beneath Searbhan's dangling clothes
to push the Giant flat upon his face.

Then seizing Searbhan's club in both his hands
three blows he struck upon the giant's head
with all the force his body could command
and soon the mighty Searbhan lay there dead.

He picked the berries 'till Grainne had her fill
then bade the warriors take some back to Fionn
and say they killed the Giant to fullfill
their wish to join the Fianna once again.

Fionn smelt the Quicken berries and he said
these berries by O'Duibhne have been picked
he's the one who killed the Giant in your stead
I am Fionn of the Fianna, and I'm not easily tricked.

Now I know where Diramaid O'Duibhne lies
I shall track him with the Fianna to his lair
and will kill this man I heartily despise
and bring his head to Tara by the hair.

Next day he rested 'neath the Quicken tree
not knowing the lovers high up rested there
although Oisin his son did not agree
Fionn set the chess board and his favourite chair.

Then Oisin sat upon the opposite seat
to seek to best his father playing chess
but Fionn with skill the younger man could beat
soon made the moves that lead him toward success.

As he looked down at the pair from up on high
O'Duibhne saw the piece for Oisin's move
and cast a Quicken berry with a sigh
that struck the piece dead centre from above.

Oisin moved the piece and won the game
and three more times the Quicken berries fell
giving him unfair advantage and the fame
of besting Fionn at chess, but Fionn could tell

no random reason caused Oisin thus to win
three straight games against a better player
"Your chance to beat me thrice was very thin,
you have been helped by the Giant's slayer".

Grainne hearing Fionn's words,shed a tear
fearing Fionn would strike her lover dead
but Diarmaid reached out and held her near
and kissed her on the lips and on her head.

Looking up Fionn saw the sweet embrace
and rising from his chair he swore an oath
he would never lightly depart from that place
before he had O'Duibhne by the throat.

Around the Quicken gathered Fionn his men
for Diamaid's head he offered many a prize
his own armour and weapons pledged he then
high rank in the Fianna would he advise.

Aonghus of the Dannaan looked in his water bowl
and saw the danger in the Quicken there
his cloak he fastened round him like a cowl
and flew to rescue those whom he held dear.

Garh of Slieve Cua climbed the branches well
but Diarmaid kicked him sharply to the ground
then as he landed Aonghus cast a spell
so he looked like Diarmaid as he came around.

A Fianna soldier severed then his head
and in that instant showed the man's true face
nine further warriors also lost their heads
as from the Quicken fell they in that place.

Then Aonghus with his cloak of magic power
whisked Grainne swift away from fear and dread
from his enemies Diarmaid would not cower
as back to Bru na Boinne Aonghus sped.

With ten dead warriors lying at his feet
Fionn was alarmed and angry past belief
he swore he would never accept defeat
and bade them all bring Diarmaid to their Chief.

Then spake brave Diarmaid from his high eerie
I will come down and fight unto the death
and many of you will perish 'ere I die
your families grieve for you beneath the earth.

Did the Fianna ever face danger without me
was I not ever first into the battle line
and left the battle last you will agree
my love for the Fianna always prime.

Oscar then approached the noble Fionn
declaring all that Diarmaid said was true
O'Duibhne was to you all but a son
forgive him now, our friendship to renew.

Fionn alas! had hardened his old heart
and would not yield an inch to Oscar's plea
forcing Oscar then to stand apart
now supporting Diarmaid totally.

Oscar climbed to the higher-most
branches offering protection to his friend
but Diarmaid sprang again high o'er the host
with Oscar springing too, his help to lend.

To Bru na Boinne both the warriors came
and under Aonghus's protection settled down
Grainne happy now her lover to reclaim
safe from the Fianna and from the angry Fionn.

Fionn now a great sea-voyage deftly planned
for Diarmaid still remained an open sore
he sought help of the King of Scotia land
who gave his sons and warriors to Fionn's war.

A thousand warriors sailed with Fionn that day
to bring Diarmaid and Oscar out to fight
for Fionn knew a geas on Diarmaid lay
to never refuse combat day or night.

The sons of the King of Scotland first came out
accompanied by their warriors heavily armed
Diarmaid and Oscar, keen to leave no doubt
slew them by the hundred, themselves unharmed.

All day the battle raged until at night
The warrior pair returned to Aonghus's house
Fionn realised that he had lost this fight
to the Land of Promise now must set his course.

He knew the only way to bring O'Duibhne down
was to bring some evil magic into play
so to the Witch his foster mother he was bound
to employ witchcraft to help him win the day.

Your enemy is mine the witch proclaimed
and soon with Fionn to Bru na Boinne sailed
a magic mist about the ship she framed
lest anyone who sought them should prevail.

Oscar had by now said his farewells
because he felt his friends would now endure
and Diarmaid daily hunted in the dells
as Grainne felt at last they were secure.

A lilly-leaf the witch now quickly sought
to turn into a millstone there and then
a round hole placed she in its centre spot
then magicked it to fly o'er hill and glen.

She found where Diarmaid hunted on a hill
and shot at him with many poisoned darts
they pierced his armour like a porcupine quill
and made his skin to burn and to smart.

Kneeling down, he took his trusty lance
and launched it at the millstone's centre hole
piercing deep the witch his only chance
and killed her dead and saved his mortal soul.

He grabbed her hair and cut off her ugly head
and brought it back to Aonghus's fireside
Aonghus burned it in molten lead,
for his foster son he felt a surging pride.

Grainne asked if this was now the end
of Fionn's pursuit to seek on them revenge
I fear said Diarmaid, Fionn will never bend
his hatred for us he will never quench.

But Aonghus felt that Fionn would now see sense
and sought an audience at the Chieftain's barque
though Fionn first bade him rudely "get thee hence"
he relented and seemed willing now to talk.

You have tried and failed to kill my foster son
and many lives of warriors have been lost
this must tire you to the very bone
and force you to consider such great cost.

Let peace between you happen once again
so all of us can turn to quiet ways
Fionn nodded his assent to Aonghus's plan
it seemed he too longed for happier days.

Then to Tara and King Cormac Aonghus went
and sought a pardon for the loving pair
The King was happy if his son consent
Cairbre felt a pardon too was fair.

Now Diarmaid sought reparations from the King
the lands in Munster that his father lost
including a donation from proud Fionn
the Leinster land of Beann Damhais as a cost,

of all the suffering forced on him of late
nor should the Fianna ever hunt these lands
nor fish there any river on his estate
nor should he or Grainne ever see their warrior bands.

At last a peace fell down upon the world
at Rath Grainne Diarmaid built a manor house
in the lands of Ceis Corann he unfurled
and sought his warlike passions there to douse.

Peace and love and much tranquility
for many years descended on the land
they lived now far from woe and enmity
they lived now just as they'd always planned.

Then one day Grainne spoke unto her man
great riches, herds, and servants have we known
but we enjoy all this while quite alone
no guest has ever entered this our home.

Maybe now's the time to make our final peace
with Fionn Mac Cumhaill, once our deadly foe
Let us prepare for him a mighty kingly feast
and with this gesture let a friendship grow.

Diarmaid felt a feast could do no harm
and invited to the feast his former friends
they hunted far and wide upon his farms
his hospitality seemed to never end.

Alas! A sad event from long time past
now intervened to change the course of time
leading to a bad and sad contrast
to the merrymaking, feasting and the wine.

When Diarmaid was a young boy wild and free
being fostered by Aonghus at the Boyne
his father Donn O'Duibhne came to see
if his foster father was keeping him in line.

Aonghus also fostered another ward
caused by the infidelity of Donn's wife
the father being Aonghus's Steward.
Donn hated his bastard son all his life.

That night a fight broke out between two hounds,
as the servant's tried to prise the dogs apart
the bastard boy twixt Donn's legs was found
hiding there lest he get ripped apart.

Donn's hatred caused him to crush the boy
to death between his powerful warrior's thighs
then flung his dead body like a toy
beneath the slavering dogs just to disguise

the commission of his wanton awful crime.
When the Steward pulled the dogs away
no mark upon the dead boy could he find
and knew that Donn had killed his boy this way.

The Steward then demanded recompense
by having Diarmaid crushed the self-same way
but Donn rose in his son's defense,
and drew his sword the Steward now to slay.

Aonghus quickly came between them both
and bade the Steward fetch at once his wand
but the steward on return swore a secret oath
and touch the wand upon the dead boy's hand.

The boy was turned into a black boar
with neither tail nor ears upon its head
and then the Steward put on it a curse
that filled the assembly there with dread.

You, Diarmaid and the Boar will live a span
which will last for exactly the same years
and when you finally die in this fair land
the boar will be cause of your wife's tears.

To lessen the force of this great curse
Aonghus put on Diarmaid a strong geas
that he must never hunt a boar
whenever on a hunt was giving chase.

While Fionn and the Fianna still enjoyed
the hospitality of the lover's manse
Diarmaid woke one night and was annoyed
he'd heard a bloodhound baying in his trance.

Grainne told him then to lie and sleep
it is a Tuatha de Danaan hound that you hear
the fairy folk hounds for their night-hunt keep
they likely hunt this night for boar and deer.

Again and again he heard the sound
throughout a restless night and at the dawn
he knew that it must be a mortal hound
It could not be a hound of the Danann.

And so he went to search through his domain
taking with him his light spear and trusty dog
though he travelled far and wide he found no game
not signs of deer or boar or wildling hog.

He climbed the height of proud Ben Bulben's head
and Fionn Mac Cumhaill alone was standing there
his men had hunted through the starry night
Ben Bulben's boar throughout its forest lair.

Diarmaid explained that wild Ben Bulben's boar
had killed each man and hound who sought its death
but the Fianna feared nothing in this world
and drove the boar toward Fionn and Diarmaid's path.

Fionn pleaded that Diarmaid leave the way
his geas forbidding him a boar to fight
but Diarmaid held his spear the boar to slay
and loosed his hound to attack with all its might.

The boar cast aside the dog like so much chaff
and Diarmaid drove his spear into its head
the boar unfazed continued its attack
as Diarmaid grabbed his sword to fight instead.

He drove the sword down hard upon its flank,
it broke in two, not causing any wound
then into Diarmaids trunk its tusks it sank
as he landed on its back, in one great bound.

It raced at pace straight down the mountainside,
halting to cast Diarmaid to the ground
then gored him savagely in his wounded side
then moved away Diarmaid once more to hound.

The boar attacked and with his failing strength
the broken sword he drove into its side
it ripped into its heart, along its length
and with a rumbling roar it finally died.

As the blood pumped from his deadly wound
Fionn approached and looked on with a grin
it pleased him to see Diarmaid on the ground
suffering for his former grievous sin.

As the Fianna warriors looked upon this scene
they were shocked that Fionn took pleasure in it all
mocking Diarmaid in his dreadful pain
he made no effort to ease his pain withal.

Your days of love and gallant deeds are o'er
you're dying now for all you did to me
I'm glad your life was ended by that boar
the anguish of my heart is now set free.

I have no need to die, said Diarmaid then
you ate the salmon of knowledge from the Boyne
a cup of water given from your hand
can restore my life, I have no need of dying.

Fionn queried why he should save his life
Diarmaid reminded Fionn how many times
in peace and many a bloody strife
to save Fionn he placed his own life on the line.

Do you not recall when at Mc Dolair's feast
Cairbre's men of Leinster fired the house
I killed half of those men before they ceased
and bringing water then the fire I doused.

Maybe so, said Fionn but that was then
since you stole my Grainne's heart from me
a trusted warrior I always saw as friend
betrayed my trust, became my enemy.

This matter was never fault of mine
since Grainne place a fearsome geas on me
and well you know I could not at any time
break such a powerful spell to set me free.

The treacherous Miodhach O Colgain
with three Kings of the fairy Underworld
who felt for you the deepest personal scorn
tried to have you killed before the dawn

at a feast at the Hostel of the Quicken Trees
he played a magic trick on you and all your men
you could not from your chairs be released
as he summoned deadly allies to the glen.

Upon your knowledge tooth you placed your thumb
which gave you warning of the traitor's plan
then sent a thought message out for me to come
to deal with the traitor O'Colgain.

I hastened to your side and blocked the ford
the three Kings must pass with their army
I filled the stream with their traitorous blood
and poured it o'er your chairs to set you free.

That night a drink you would have given me
go to yon spring and bring one to me here
forget our quarrel, this once let it be
without it I will die I strongly fear.

Fionn shook his head, as Oscar softly knelt
he cradled Diarmaid's head upon his knee
on his face was etched what he now felt
life was ebbing from Diramaid steadily.

To Fionn now Oscar spoke, sat on the ground
in your cupped hands bring water to my friend
then Fionn denied that water could be found
but Oscar pointed to the Spring at footpath's end.

Fionn with bad grace went down to the stream
and filled his cupped hands with the healing draught
yet thinking back at all that once had been
he let water fall through his fingers on the path.

Twice he let this happen as he walked
though Oscar accused him loudly of bad faith
the third time just before he baulked
Diarmaid died and then it was too late.

The Fianna gathered Diarmaid's body round
and gave three great cries of mourning for his fate
Oscar laid Diarmaid's head upon the ground
and railed at Fionn for causing Diarmaid's death.

To kill Fionn Mac Cumhaill, Oscar drew his sword
but Oisin grasped him tightly by the hand
there has been enough death upon this sward
enough sadness now will fall upon the land.

Fionn held Mac an Chuill, Diarmaid's faithful hound
as to Bru na Boinnne all that day they tread
an anxious Grainne at Aongus's cave they found
waiting news of Diarmaid with some dread.

On seeing Mac an Chuill held fast by Fionn
she knew her husband Diarmaid now was dead
she fell into a swoon upon the ground
as Oscar bore her to her marriage bed.

When Fionn told her the place that Diarmaid died
she sent her servants there to bring him home
but Aonghus was already by his side
with three hundred warriors of Tuatha Danaan.

They bore Diarmaid home upon their shields
and at Bru na Boinne built a golden bier
which they carried on their shoulders to a field
and buried Diarmaid holding back their tears.

Grainne mourned O Duibhne all her life
and never married any man again
no one would ever have her as a wife
the death of Diarmaid brought her too much pain.

REFLECTIONS

The world does seem to be, in the words of my friend from Louisiana, "going to hell in a hand-basket", and now and then the enormity of humanity's lack of understanding of its venality and complicity in the destruction of the natural world bothers even a poet.

REFLECTIONS

Years pass and blend
and draw in nigh the future
where dreams and fears contend
for signs of saner times.
Suspicion and mistrust stalk every land
burying decency and common sense
in oil thick, pestilential greed,
against which lies no real defence.
Common sense,
stares fixedly, on evil riding by
yet numbed by greed
turns ever a blind eye.

Self-interest ever beckons toward the cold
the negative, destructive side of being,
more convenient and ego-feeding right,
denying in a rash of foolish pride
the burgeoning anger of the world
so long forgotten and so in need of light.

Will only cataclysms qualify
to breach the damn of all pervading vice
or nature all at once her power apply
to batter home the lesson in a thrice,
to the venal, and vainglorious,
who can but now rely

on an insane philosophy
re-cloaked in hedonistic humbug,
an ignoble intellectual discourse,
clinging to the tattered remnant
of a Guidon lost in battle
displayed for the admiration of a mob.

Are we to be the better intellect
evidence of a cosmic consciousness
in a spinning sentient orb
or a mere speck of endearing dirt
irritating the finger of the Lord.

Every morning, as I drove into work, on the North Quays in Dublin, I saw four winos, three men and one woman sitting on a street corner, just off the main road, probably having just been let out of a night shelter. I decided to give them each a personality and a history. I met the great Ronnie Drew once in Temple Bar at the invitation of a mutual acquaintance. He was looking for material for an LP he was planning, and I gave him this poem. He asked his son Phelim, an actor, to read it and we met again a couple of weeks later. Ronnie reckoned that Phelim liked the poem and said to his Dad "Jaysus, Dad, this is powerful stuff. Does that fella write plays"!! Other than Prof Kennelly, this is the only comment my poems have received.

THE STREET PARTY

Eight o'clock in the morning, I assume my accustomed place
four from the left in line, back arched against the pebble-dash wall
yards from the bellow of the North Dublin Quays.
There's a chill in the morning mist, etched on the condensed breath
of the City's comfortable citizenry, indulging their daily progress
from warm hearth to warm desk, bellies distended with rich victuals,
none past their sell-by date. I hunger.
There's a gap where the last flagon of cider permeated my system
blotting out reality, and the mundane misery
of cloying crushing circumstance.

I feel an elbow in my ribs, jarring my harrowing hangover,
as second place from the left is filled with Jemser's jovial jug.
Clad by the Simon Community, in everything but manners,
he is the warmer for it, though not in disposition or intent,
his gulping bites, at a chip-filled roll, belch a gangrenous greeting,
giving halitosis a bad name.
A man of lineage fallen from grace, he is at ease with poetry or
prostitutes
the latter more Benburb street than Fitzwilliam in more halcyon
times.

He's sick but cares not a damn, since death is a friend long awaited
whose mad mauvais methods detain him at a diffident distance,
'til the Simon coat slips from his shivering frame, at dead of numbing
night,
offering Hypothermia another inglorious victim.

Johnny sails into sight, grimace set in stygian stubble,
no philosopher this, or lover of poetic paeans,
he is a practised vulgarian, seeing no sense in civilization.
A chameleon worshipper of chaos, ranting and roaring his ire
at organised religion and the smugness of settled society.
So often seen staggering the centre of the road,
or intent on minding the middle of a four-lane,
he's battered, blood-stained and scarred
from a plethora of arguments, with Quixotic adversaries.
Nursing two fresh lesions, boasted like heraldic honours,
he totters tipsily to the third paved station,
warming his ire in our collective misery.

Next to come sweet Bridget, adding tone and temperament
to our vainglorious Valhalla.
Her affability in adversity, her patience in the face of paucity,
her insight, in the midst of insanity, her stoic good humour,
in the face of horror, her gentleness in the face of brutality,
shines through the booze, the glue and the drugs
like a Paschal candle in a deserted Easter Cathedral.
She told me she had no memory of family,
but those who do, and they are few
say she bore a low and lonely estate.
She seeks the fourth place, subsiding into its familiarity
like an old raddled barge on the Grand Canal,
distressed, dissolute, dispirited, licking her liberal lacerations
in the fractious friendship, of our garrulous gargoyle gathering.

We are a cabal of calcified cadavers, in a twilight world
slipping and sliding between a partly perceived reality
and a covenant of constant confusion.
Purloined of purpose, milked of meaning,
and so it seems to the casual observer.
But we recall the pressure of settled life,
the cloying, clammy, sameness of rancid routine,
the never-ending demands of daily toil,
the tyranny of tolls and taxes, and myriad demands,
driving us inexorably, tumbling through alcohol's anodyne door,
into the waiting arms of calm oblivion, coaxing and courting us,
with the cerebral subtlety of a whore, intent on all we possess,
drowning us in a liquid libidinous lake
of the overpowering ordure of self-pity.

We part-happy band have retreated like the whipped lemming legions
of a haughty General, running scared
from the all-conquering curse of modern life.
We have rejected rechauffe reality, designed by demented despots,
and embraced our imperfect shifting shanty town imperfection,
erected on sand, never conceived to endlessly endure.
Mired in misanthropic minatory misery, circled by cold,
humbled by hunger, festooned with fetid festering filth,
the early morning Street party is our touchstone, talisman and link
with what residual reality there is, in an unforgiving driven world.
It is our personal Pitcairn, and we have long since immolated
our means of escape, with relentless reckless relish.

The Street Party is complete, we four comfortable and content
amid the discomfort of our happy huddling from the dank
morning mist,
know this state has lingered longer than our befuddled brains
can grasp.

Together in the half-light, we trade fables of frenetic foraging,
for the basics, rejoicing in the crumbs cascading from rich tables,
welfare, volunteers, charities and do-good-folk,
providing us with one good square a day,
when we deign to desert the flagon of golden glory,
scrounged, stolen or swapped.
Stark warnings haunt the idiocy our ramblings,
as with sweet Bridget, when she wastes meagre resources
on glue and drugs, and we rescue her in the nick of time,
from cruel Charons's grasp, a crazed and frightened child,
grim reminder of our pathetic perilous plight.
Yet we lack the will to change, abuse has robbed our reason,
we drift in destructive, dreary desperation
wishing the Grim Reaper, to confer compassion one sub-zero night,
when dense with drink, we succumb, slipping silently into oblivion,
no longer burdening the bemused citizens of Anna Livia's littoral.

Dilemma

You are precious and desired, so small and so vulnerable,
I am your protector, my love for you began
before you existed, the expression of another love
presaging your growth within me.
Your heartbeat is mine, I sense the primordial bond,
straddling aeons of time, an outpouring of oneness
and avalanche of joy, tinged with sadness,
from the dark scientific certainty
that your developing strength, can, one day, destroy me.
It seems you will develop into a less than perfect being,
ever dependent upon the good-will and charity
of inevitable indifference.
I face conflicting choices, to simply sacrifice myself
(greater love than this?),
gifting you an indifferent existence, that may not long endure,
or snuffing out your tomorrows in selfish preservation.
A megaton of pros and cons parade themselves before me
with the stinging clarity of a sword-thrust to the heart,
nor do I lack conflicting urgings to impale myself
on either horn of this appalling dilemma,
on which I must, with doubtful dignity, transfix myself and soon.
What casts me down so low, is the barnacled conviction
that this damnable decision, is mine and mine alone,
nothing and no one, however caring and well-meaning
can lift this leaden limpet-mine from my shell-shocked shoulders.
I pray that you will forgive me, when the awesome moment comes
for as surely as the Universe revolves, whichever course I set,
will steer me to the unsafe harbour of a truly personal Hell!!

Some years ago, when I was involved in building a sea-fed oil terminal in New Ross, Co Wexford for a company called Campus Oil, I bought a mobile home from a former boarding school pal. The site of the terminal was filled with quarry material by a company owned by a local character, called Tom Walsh. There was an old Anglo-Irish 250 acre estate outside the town, I think called Oak Park . In the late fifties, the elderly couple, who owned it, died, and their son came back from England to finalise matters. The local story is that he burned a lot of old family correspondence in the main fireplace one night, and apparently fell asleep, in an armchair in front of the fire, whereupon the whole place burnt down, leaving only four columns, that once graced the entrance, standing. Tom Walsh bought the estate, bulldozed the remains of the mansion into the cellars and built a three bedroomed bungalow on top. Tom let me park my mobile home in front of the house, where I lived happily for two years, whilst building the terminal. I often ruminated on the old Anglo-Irish ascendency family who originally occupied the house.

Ascendency

Doric columns, stark against a brooding sky
tenuous testimony to a grander age,
held fast by granite lintels
carved and polished,
with the lost artistry of yesteryear.
A lonely vigil, void of meaning,
old glory, burned and brought to earth,
life and purpose ruined,
where once was laughter,
music too, if only for the few,
daily bustle of a noble See,
and endless preparations
for the next soiree,
enjoyed beneath the depressive threat
of dour disgruntled peasantry.

Strange abuse of power and privilege
now brought low,
a level place,
save Doric columns
stark against a brooding sky.

I visited the former concentration camp twice and was struck on both occasions by the complete lack of bird song in that awful place.

BERGEN BELSEN

No bird-song breaks the silence
of Bergen Belsen's mounds
eerie stillness wraps a shroud
around its baleful bounds.
"Fumtzig Tausend Tot" here
"Hundert Tausend Tot" there
mute mimes in graven granite
scar the lacerated landscape.
The verdant capping sward
screams silently of old infamity
and cloaks a charnel house
marking a very human sin,
unshrivable, save by the dead.

The leaden languid lanes
like Ossuaries of shame,
drive knarled nails in memories
paralysed by pain.
Tsunamies of grief ooze from the ground
trailing waves of woe in their wake,
"Fumtzig Tausend Tot" here
"Hundert Tausend Tot" there,
a haunting numeral earthquake,
memorialising the snuffed-out souls
of angels brutalised to oblivion,
by encompassing depravity of evil ghouls.

No bird song breaks the silence
of Bergen Belsen's mounds.

MUSIC

When dull discordant interludes invade,
my mind will ever seek the mother-lode
of precious Polyhymnia's caress
and soothing unguents by her hand bestowed.
Though furies rage unchecked within my heart
and anger levy war upon my soul,
yet paramount she claims her cherished place
her soothing calming balm a brimming bowl.
While in a river torrent swept along
by swirling forces, passively perceived,
benign my journey on from placid pools,
to dancing rapids' frenzy unrelieved;
crescendo spent, surrenders up her crown,
and on my souls light side is tumbled down.

I'm sure all of us have met someone who is so patently good, it makes you wonder what happened to original sin. I knew such a person, whose patent goodness was a life-long indication that I am simply not the Christian I would like to be.

In the presence of Goodness

Each word, each movement, or gesture
confuses and hurts, as I see
the sort of Christian person
I should aspire to be.
I wonder if this is a naive soul
serene in simplistic belief,
a celibate, guileless creature
a stranger to normal grief.

Lost in the pure and the simple,
transported by transcendent love,
orphaning me with goodness,
draining my will, my resolve.
Am I better for this encounter
with a patently powerful force,
irrevocably changed and affected,
revision my only recourse?

No! I'll cling to my dissolute credo,
it's a comfort and I can't afford
to replace my cynical outlook
with an organised view of the Lord!
After all His message was simple,
"Love each other, as I have loved you",
my mistrust of organised credos
is a faith I will never eschew.

By nature I am not a pacifist. There are principles worth fighting for, but the Iraq war, never mind it was against an obvious despot, was started for a false reason, at the wrong time, against the wrong people, in the wrong place. Richard Nixon took America off the gold standard in 1973, because he got oil producers to agree to denominate all oil deals in dollars. George Bush, and Tony Blair knew what they were doing and did it anyway, because Saddam Hussein felt powerful enough to threaten to denominate all his oil sales in Euros or Roubles, threatening the Petro-dollar.

THE UNJUST WAR

Just War, the execution of a Criminal
or self defence,
those Cathechism rules,
were broken anyway, and
by the latest convert to the faith.
After, he defended himself,
with mendacious mealy mouth,
as the Cathechism rang in my ears.
He spoke of great dangers
of WMD no one could find,
as disruptive-pattern uniforms
were gashed to shreds
on roads heavily mined,
amid the charnel-house that was Baghdad.
He talked of a better times
as another shaped device
pierced the body armour of a tank crew,
exposing the futility of their sacrifice
in this Pyrrhic victory of the mind.

He spoke of the pride of a great nation
its soul already pawned to another
this once, and never to be again, King,

talking to deafened ears
on a blood stained, bombed-out
pavement, in a far off country.
He spoke of his own greed,
his impotent slavery
to a once conquered colony,
while mired in self-interest
and over-weaning pride.

WMD – Weapons of Mass Destruction

This poem was prompted by an acrimonious discussion with a highly intelligent friend, who had the ability to look at the crumbling economic eco-space we humans currently occupy, leaving millions of poor and indigent people in its wake, and see no reason whatever to change the preposterous paradigm that led us here.

THE TIME OF RECKONING

I advocated change to an educated man
rich in letters and this worlds goods
as we ground our way through the news
of the globe's gloomy miseries
crammed relentlessly and ruthlessly
into the well-paid maw
of a largely uncritical media.
I forced my mind to journey
back into the mists of time
finding a gentler, less hurried era
where intellectual discourse dwelt
in more accessible places,
where people lived in frugal harmony,
not necessarily in agreement,
yet holding fast to a sense of society.
I long for robust debate
without the acrimony of winning
or the need to crush opponents
eradicating their meaningful place
in the search for intellectual honesty.
I mourn the dread demands
of corrupting commerce run rampant
shorn of check, balance or conscience,
bestriding a poverty of ideas
like a Colossus.

We congratulate ourselves of late
that we got here on the shoulders of giants;
where are the giants now,
as pygmies, in thrall to Mammon,
wearing well-cut suits,
shirk their responsibilities
and mortgage their morals
to the fat and indolent moguls of the Earth,
intent on despoiling our children's heritage,
consigning divine oversight to irrelevance.
A change must come; we have passed
the day of reckoning, mewling and puking
like spoiled brats, over escalating demands,
for toys we have not the intelligence
to understand or play with.
Mother Nature will assert her rightful place
against the mounting stupidities of the race.

I have followed his career for some time now and watched him descend into a morass of dangerous sycophancy and serial mendacity. He poses a clear and present danger to the world in my humble opinion.

Mediocrity and Power

Intellectually impoverished, narrow, blustering, bombastic,
a caricature strutting the political stage like a demented gnome
devoid of honour, in pawn to powerful interest,
a mundane morality mostly concerned with wealth
Covid graveyards overflowing with the insanity of his sloth.
Inarticulate ramblings replace statesmanship
reduce diplomatic discourse to cant and caterwauling
replace truth with myriad fantasies mouthed to air
insult faith with a brandished never read Bible
as Evangelicals laud a stance delivering meagre return
from an empty vessel enamoured of its own dull sound.
A once proud nation is duped by impotent mediocrity
while the violent vote filled fringe is courted incessantly
and inarticulate rage is vented on new fangled media
displaying a dogged determination to eschew advice
other than self-serving numbingly narrow focus.
The revolving door of his office fills with rolling heads
as he cravenly pursues conflict rather than compromise
driving a great nation against its best interest into the maw of Mars
dragging the once free world in his dangerous devilish wake.

I suppose everyone, when they reach a certain age, reflects on their mortality. It happened to me in my fifties. Never mind all the talk about 70 being the new 50. Who knows how long the merry-go-round ride is going to last.

SWAN SONG

In the twilight of my life
what might have been looms large,
a feeling of what I might have done
if I had taken charge.
in times of high emotion
fuelling love and high ambition
those heady highs and failures
when success was an obsession.
Will I settle into quietude
the calm of dotage years
while watching funereally
the exit of my peers,
or will I look into the mirror
not see the ravages of time
an un-graceful descent into
a frightening paradigm.
I think now of an old man
who told me one fine day
that his head remained a youngster
while his body ceased to play,
like a child trapped in a vessel
decayed from overuse,
while its young and active mind
kept agile, free and loose.
His wisdom struck a chord with me
for I've never felt so live
as when I look at all the love

which helped me to survive.
The timbre of sweet laughter,
of grand-kids, family, friends
pierce the fog of introspection
and set one on the mend
reviving all that's best in life
in its meandering melee
as I seek to sing my swansong
in a sweeter, higher key.

I wrote this in a melancholic booze-soaked mood and was a little surprised to find it vaguely coherent when I sobered up.

EULOGY

Close not the curtains on my life
let the light stream in,
purple not the mirrors or the art
lay out the whiskey and the gin,
let friend and foe alike rejoice
I am past tense now
sorrow cannot change my fate
as I take my final bow.
Life is where conflict dwells
I have left all that behind
said my last farewells,
my exit pass is signed.
Mine has been a busy life
triumph and failure filled
love and heartache in their turn
have rendered all their bills.
Mars and Mammon have I served
in full and faithful measure
but children and un-stinted love
have been my greatest treasure
And now I've gone to face the Lord,
and answer for my sins
another great adventure
in eternity begins.

Humour

Humour has played a huge part in my life. I relish a well told story, a neatly crafted joke, with the unexpected punch line, brilliant situation comedy, the craft of truly gifted comedians. Life would be dull indeed without humour. The sharp minded will note the homage to the bard.

HUMOUR

Give me those of humour, bright hearts and laughing eyes,
who brighten up the dullest day, with candid, cheering cries,
who tell an oft-heard story as though it were their own,
words tripping lightly off their tongues,
like speech were theirs alone.
Their creative crafted cadences, like scintillating wine,
a honeyed discourse challenging the slothful lapse of time.
It's easy to court misery, calamity, distress,
and never raise a grateful gaze, to life's lithe loveliness;
but lucky for us smiling souls, are placed along the way,
to teach us to be joyful and hold the gloom at bay,
to tempt us from our torment, and inward-looking mores
and lead the way through laughter to happy shining shores,
where mirthful fun and gaiety, and merry-making sport,
replace the languid legacy of Melancholy's Court.

Some year's ago I supervised the building of, and subsequently managed, a sea-fed Oil Terminal, for Campus Oil in New Ross, County Wexford. I was occasionally summoned to head office in Dublin, and, on the way up through Wexford, I passed a 2 acre field, which, in season, was covered in strawberries. I used to buy two baskets-full, one of which I left with my Mother in Tullow, Co Carlow, and the other I consumed in its entirety before I got to Dublin.

Strawberry Fever

In my saner moments I'm a Stoic, but I become a rash and
sinful Epicure,
when the Strawberries are ripe, I become the gorging type,
and stuff them down my gullet by the score.
They're so tempting red and juicy, I feel I haven't done my duty,
'till I've eaten every punnet in my reach,
as the juice runs down my chin, I know that gluttony's a sin
and in Hell the Devil's carving out my niche.
County Wexford is to blame, they're growing strawberries again,
and resisting them would be too great a trial
there are other ways I say, if for sin you have to pay,
you can wear hair shirts, not practice self-denial.
It happens every year, when the strawberries are here
I can't help straying from the narrow path,
yet, I feel the Lord, when he made the strawberry sward
He made allowances for Strawberry psychopaths.

While proceeding down the Quays, in Dublin, one day, I was held up at a traffic light by a Lady who I immortalised in this modest verse.

ESSENTIAL REPAIRS

Oh! God look at those eye-brows,
they haven't been plucked in years,
perhaps I should try a false eye-lash,
where's my tissue, those mascara smears.
Dear Lord, are those lines at the sides of my eyes,
is a face-lift the only way out,
it's this mirror, it isn't one bit clean
or maybe it's just when I pout.
Who are those eejits looking at me
Mmmm! I like the one with the pipe,
Oh! hell, my face is beginning to sag,
and my skin looks like two pounds of tripe.
Why is he shaking his fist at me?,
my hair's in a terrible mess
I think I'll get it cut shorter to-day,
but no!, there'd be less to caress,
Merciful heaven, that chap's started to shout
he's looking particularly mean,
good God, I'm sitting in traffic,
how long have those lights been turned green!!??

Sandymount strand, in South Dublin, is a haunt for lovers.

SANDYMOUNT STRAND

The cars in the car park at Sandymount Strand
in the hours after midnight have passed,
seem to take on an animate life of their own
leaving passers-by somewhat aghast.

Their windows steam up like a kettle,
and water runs down them like rain,
as they lurch and rock from side to side
like a beached whale in serious pain.

Then they bounce up and down with great vigour
like a fat jolly man when he laughs,
and the windows, sometimes, wind down on their own,
and you'd swear you could hear the car gasp.

Although there's no sign of an owner
that the car seems alive there's no doubt,
perhaps is fresh air and sea water
that cause's their jiggling about.

They always provoke prurient interest
and excite each voyeur in the place
while sweet old ladies smother their eyes
and declare the whole thing a disgrace.

"Cars were never designed for such work
that requires them to grunt and to squeal,
if the good Lord intended that carry-on,
He'd have given a Four Poster wheels"!!

I was amused one day while driving in the inevitable traffic jam, at the antics of a couple in a car behind me. The lady seemed to have gotten up on the wrong side of the bed that day.

THE REAR-VIEW MIRROR

The sights in one's rear view mirror, are a feature of modern life,
like the car being driven by a husband, flanked by a
cross-looking wife.
In the back are two churlish children, giving vent with
venomous lungs,
while the wife's working up to a frenzy, and sharpening the
edge of her tongue.

Madam's clearly not pleased about something, that he's done or
should not have done,
but the problem's about to be sorted, and guess who's going
to be stung.
In a rare pause he turns to confront her, but she bites off his nose
with a bark
and the look of the hunted suffuses his face, as his day turns a
deep shade of dark.

He tries once more to placate her, but selects the wrong gear
in the car,
which stalls in the midst of the traffic, and this further fuels the war.
I read his lips as he mutters, "Look what you made me do now,"
her reply does little to settle, the furrows ploughed deep in his brow.

Then she rounds on the kids in the back-seat, for no one escapes
this harangue,
then returns re-invigorated to husband, with the full range of sharp
tooth and fang,

I can only surmise what has happened, but one thing I'm bound
to relate,
I'm glad it's him and not me, that's suffering this harrowing fate.

As a plethora of similar playlets, entertain me in traffic to-day,
it strikes me that having the wife in the car, is too high a price to pay,
for the doubtful joys of marriage, and the comfort of a connubial bed,
that form of refined car-borne torture, would fill poor Goliath
with dread.

I have lived in a lot of houses in several continents and always revelled in their different characters and the way they had knack of shaping one's thinking about life in small ways. They all had a distinct aroma, which I celebrate here.

Houses

Each house has got a character, but more than that, a smell
a quite distinct aroma, that anyone can tell,
denotes that house and it alone from others of its kind
no matter how constructed, with its destiny entwined.
Some get it from their newness and augment it through the years,
while some reflect their owners, whether commoners or peers.
Others stem from subtle blends of things that fill the pot,
each kitchen manufacturing its own forget-me-not.
Though some repel, yet you can tell, some powerfully attract,
their rose perfume in every room, delights the nasal tract.
The smells of friends on odd weekends were always a delight,
and what of new-wed couples with the nappy war to fight,
or the girlfriend's home, where one bemoans her parents'
strict regime
a fresh bouquet on every day, suffused its settled scene
and the homes of older couples, such as grandparents and such
emit elusive essences that warn one not to rush.
Those pallid artificial scents, dispensed now from a can,
beside home's nurturing nosegay, appear but pale and wan,
and none I'm sure gainsay the fact, that houses live and breathe
a world without their pot-pourri, can scarcely been conceived.

I was a Director of a small company situated on the north Quays in Dublin and just across the road was the new Dublin Corporation, building built by the then "flavour of the month" architect, Sam Stephenson, who also designed the old Central Bank building in Dame Street. This is a reflection of a day I spent with a bad hangover.

A BAD DAY ON THE QUAYS

I traverse the day, on the end of a hangover,
gathered in the night in Temple Bar.
I sit, bleary-eyed, at my lamp-lit desk,
overlooking the traffic-choked Quays,
pondering Sam Stephenson's Dublin,
as he told me once it would be called,
staring rudely in my window, in its Maginot-line ugliness.
The No 39 Bus blares bad-temperately at me
resenting my prurient interest in the blond gracing its upper deck.
I cannot focus my tumbled thoughts, or grieve for the pink docket,
festooning my illegally parked naughty Nissan,
lonely in its side road, where it sought to hide,
from the yellow-black storm troopers,
intent on piling ruin on my day.
I will endure and later, when evening dulls my aches,
and the debilitating diurnal of commanding commerce,
rescue my Jovial Japanese chariot
and weave a circuitous route
to avoid the men in blue, guardians of the bilious bag,
expressing unseemly interest in my nocturnal foray.

But first at lunch hour for the craic, I'll stir myself from stasis,
for the sake of my sanity, and gravitate to Grafton Street,
paying homage en route to bronzed Molly Malone,
still burdened with her wheelbarrow, magnet for teeming tourists

112

mobbing Trinity's environs, and the roar of Dame Street's traffic.
I will tread my way through a cacophony of street-wise urchins,
pavement artists and musical misfits, before coming to rest
behind a satisfying, steaming, salacious, Bewley's coffee,
accessory after the fact to delicious Fusco comestibles,
a cause of confession, if ever there was one.
Cheered, I will negotiate, the new-fangled Dublin left bank,
home to the trendy, and the trite, as only Temple Bar can be,
still pleasant in its cobble-stoned, lamp-lit old-world confusion
but streets ahead of its former vacant site-like decay.

The afternoon seems different, with the busy Garda Truck Crane,
harvesting its latest crop of urban-clearway-parked Culchies,
up for the day, and oblivious of Corporation demands
signalled in double yellow lines meeting on the horizon.
Their haste to snap up riotous reductions
in the Capel Street and Henry Street bazaars,
blind them to city-slicker demands, unheard of in Culchieland.
Beside me, a builder intensifies his efforts to discomfit all,
as he valiantly mans the pumps, to prevent Anna Livia
inundating Frank Feeley's pride and joy.

The sight of all that water, makes me dream of Bongo Ryans,
and the best measure of the dark demonic brew,
as a bad day on the Quays shows signs of getting better
and all is not entirely lost.

Culchie – rude Dublin word for countryfolk
Frank Feeley – former head of Dublin Corporation

This poem needs no introduction but arose from a visit to a supermarket in Dublin in the early eighties.

QUEUES

I hate queuing for any reason,
but reserve the highest level
of periodic paranoia
for queuing in Supermarkets.
As a male, I have already suffered enough,
wandering overburdened aisles
like a lost and sorrowing soul,
commenting to unfindable attendants,
"Ok! I give up, where is it this week!"
I'm not in pursuit of exotics
just simple staples of life-support
which have attracted the gimlet eye
of the inscrutable marketing man,
bent on dicing with male shoppers'
finely balanced pysches.
Besides the fruitless foraging,
there is endless trolley twanging
by female tyrants, trailing ankle biters
pouting piercing demands,
unplanned for in the budget,
noisily in their wake.

Just when you have run to ground
a longed for strawberry jam,
a four wheeled wire Exocet missile,
with independently targeted castors,
like a malevolent robot,
screams past, with banshee screeches,

114

designed to unhinge a guru.
This weekly raucous ritual
renders rough men rudderless,
as they moor at the check-out
to wait in interminable line,
and fall beneath the baleful gaze
of the checker of provender,
whose role in life is to frustrate
obfuscate and procrastinate,
like some SS-majorette.
"Did you weigh this, that's a leaker
those are four for a Euro,
do you have your loyalty card
bags are 50 cents each",
she intones like a broken record.

In desperation the weak desert
and join another line
shorter and three aisles away,
but are beaten to the draw,
by overladen ladies
behind mountainous trolleys,
designed for relieving famine
of African proportions.
If the lifts don't work
my cup will overflow with bile,
and sure enough they don't,
testing further my faith
in a Divine providence,
to Whom, tomorrow, Sunday
I will offer these tribulations,
for the betterment of my soul,
in that future Nirvana,

where Queues require
a permit from a merciful Almighty,
who, in temper, I recall,
broke up a Queue at the Temple,
because it was,
an Abomination in His sight.

I lived in College Grove, Castleknock some years ago and outside my house was a large green space. Without warning, one day, Dublin Corporation put in a lovely scalloped patch of greenery, flowers and trees, which quite beautified the area directly in front of my house. A neighbour of mine, Fonsie Condon, a man with proverbial green fingers, took a proprietary interest in this patch and kept it looking beautiful for no recompense whatsoever. He also stole my lawnmower and never gave it back, but compensated by cutting my grass.

ODE TO FONSIE CONDON

I don't know why the Corporation planted trees before my house,
generosity was never their strong suit,
their usual operation is more prevarication,
they're never tempted down the speedy route.
Yet, a sweeping sylvan scene, in various shades of green,
an arboreal extravagance of note,
quite suddenly appeared, I thought it rather weird,
as spontaneous eruption seemed remote.

At this juncture, may I say, their entered into play,
with affinity to Nature seldom seen,
my neighbour Fonsie Condon, who with reckless gay abandon
took a fancy to the forest quite obscene.
It's not that I'd complain of a gift horse in the main,
or cavil at the goods the Fates might bring
I could even express pleasure, in no uncertain measure,
but Fonsie Condon says he owns the bloody thing.

I'm not the greatest gardener, I can vouch with candour,
and don't possess green fingers, by the way,
I'm practical and sane, don't like to tax my brain,
I let Mother Nature always have her say.
But when the Corporation abandoned their plantation,

117

without a though for further nurturing,
I'm sure they'd heard the story, and didn't need to worry,
they knew Condon thought he owned the bloody thing.

He's a dedicated digger, and pursues with vim and vigour,
any weed that tries to show above the ground,
in sunshine, snow or hail, he pursues the holy grail,
of keeping Mother Nature trussed and bound.
This attitude has strayed to every flower and blade
or leaf that tends to lack strong discipline,
this crusade he follows through towards the forest too,
'cause Fonsie Condon thinks he owns the bloody thing.

Showing weather rank disdain, with no regard for pain,
or fatigue that other mortals are prey to,
he forks and hoes and rakes, he says for all our sakes,
and by his efforts furnishes a view,
of arboreal delight, of which I alone have sight
it would grace the palace gardens of a King,
yet still I can't enjoy, what should delight the eye
'cause Fonsie Condon says he owns the bloody thing.

Last night when walking by, I heard him heave a sigh,
while grovelling on his knees among the weeds,
he muttered "I'm a fool, Mahon's sitting in the cool,
while I'm attending to the forest's needs,
"Why can't the swine arise, give us all a big surprise,
lazy neighbours like that blackguard ought to swing".!
I said I'd love to help, the complaining culchie whelp,
if Fonsie Condon didn't own the bloody thing!!

The Coronavirus was still raging while I wrote these. I was staring out the window one beautiful South African Evening, in lockdown, when I was hit by the funny side of that tragic event, then the prayer occurred to me.

CORONA MUSING

Enormous white clouds
in a red-tinged evening
revive the wanderlust in me,
a shackled surrogate
tethered and in thrall,
to a micro-organism
locking me down
as tight as a fishes bum
and that's watertight.
And that's not all, as I realise
there is no visible end
to this interminable incarceration
of the entire nation
while we listen to the deep-freeze burp
and the double fridge slurp
from over-loading
brought on by binge shopping
at a Mall crammed by frightened lunatics
who shortly will be barred
in their personal bedlam
festooned with toilet rolls
and enough bread to feed
Ethiopia in its darkest hour.

Prayer

C alm your mind and soul
O ne thing alone is sure
R elief comes only from the Lord
O nly he provides the cure
N ever doubt His Divine love
A nd trust in His great power

V erily comes he to our aid
I n this our darkest hour
R ely always upon his grace
U nburden your immortal soul
S oon the Lord will show his face
And lead His children to their goal

They embrace all genders of this modern world, and most of us have encountered one.

The Shrew

No one else in all the world
annoys me more than you,
your whinging, cringing, carping ways
the hallmark of the Shrew.
Your wizened nature has not been
produced alone by chance,
its warped and twisted humours
no random circumstance.
For rarely in this wayward world
can anyone each day,
start out at morn to wail and moan,
and hold at once at bay
imagined insults, large and small
and slights of every kind,
inflicted on your tortured heart
by a convoluted mind.
You paint a broad scenario
inhabited by ghouls
or sycophants, and egotists
and ill-intentioned fools,
whose sole intent is to disrupt
the perfect world you've made,
their ill-intention little more
than a comical charade,
while never pausing to reflect
that maybe you're the one
returning mirror images
of all that you have done,

to sour and scar and mark and mar
in endless waves of strife,
while one brief brush with Charity
would illuminate your life.

In the era of Coronavirus conspiracy theories are rife; not that they weren't so before but they reached a new crescendo at this time.

CONSPIRACY THEORIST

I ate a Conspiracy theorist to-day,
'cause of his salty tales,
I felt he went right off the tracks
or fell between the rails.
He tasted far worse than I thought,
stringy and too tough,
so I added pepper to his stew,
because I'd had enough,
of Bill Gates and the Clintons
and all those microchips,
who assassinated Kennedy
and got De Lorean in the shit.
As I stirred this pot and added leaks
that came from the Pentagon
I pondered how that flag still waved
with Apollo eleven on the moon.
Have the Area 51 boys
really flown to the stars
and is it true that Monica Lewinsky
really didn't like cigars!
Was John F Kennedy really shot
by Geoffrey Damer's mum
and did Teddy really ever go
on that Chappaquiddick run.
After this I had the hiccups
as a bone stuck in my throat
and if you believe all this crap
you're clearly far too young to vote.

I wrote this poem to entertain my two boys, who grew up in urban environments and had little exposure to the country delights I enjoyed as a boy.

THE FOX

I saw that fox again to-day as it slinked across the field,
he paused beside a hedgerow as a badger made him yield
as ever food was on his mind and it wasn't far away,
the Farmer's tasty chickens were his primary prey to-day.

The browny russet colours in his splendid coat of fur,
shining brightly in the sunlight, as he ran, became a blur,
in and out of teeming thickets, under briar and over stump,
he paused warily to sniff the air, between each skip and jump.

With ears pricked up and nose alert, silently he moved,
was that danger up ahead, he thought, rustling in the wood,
but no!, the wind was playing tricks, and off he went again
as darkening clouds crossed the sky, promising certain rain.

A tree blown down by raging storms, in Winter long ago,
now formed a permanent bridge, across a streams swift flow
and on the other side of it, high wire ran round a yard,
securing clucking chickens from the fangs of feared Reynard.

A cock strode by with gimlet eye, to see that all was well,
his breast stuck out, without a doubt, no finer sentinel,
with soldiers gait, he patrolled the fate, of all within his view,
that danger lurked outside the fence, was something he well knew.

The Fox was woefully worried, he knew that cock of old,
if he crossed the tree, the cock would see, no point in being bold.
He thought of swimming over, but the stream was cold and wide,
and he'd surely get his brush wet, crossing that divide.

He sniffed the air from his temporary lair, but the wind was
strong alas!,
"I'll have to keep downwind" he thought, crouched there in the grass.
He wondered how, with puckered brow, and then, to his relief,
three cows strolled by, and blocked the sky, with ample sides of beef.

The rooster now unsighted, Fox sped across the tree
and slipped behind a low furze bush, to view his enemy.
Phase one complete, a major feat, in manner he approved ,
cold cunning brought him closer to the dinner he most loved.

With sudden dread the cock stopped dead; he peered right
through the wire,
his comb stuck up, his wings spread out, in fighting fit attire.
The chickens stopped their clucking, their heads came up as one,
looking at their protector, as he neared the fence alone.

"Reynard's out there, we'd best take care" he clucked in urgent tone
while searching every blade of grass, and scanning every stone.
The Fox laid low in the field below, and hardly dared to breathe,
till the cock relaxed and turned about, and the chickens took his lead.

The heat now off, he'd had enough of waiting for his prey,
the time had come to make his run, and proudly win the day.
He scurried round the chicken house, and burrowed in the ground,
at a place behind that wooden shed, he knew was far from sound.

The planking gave for our hunter brave, and in he stuck his snout,
quite unprepared he furiously stared at what pranced there all about.
A single fluffy day-old chick, stood right before his eyes,
completely calm, without a qualm, displaying no surprise.

Before the fox could make a move, the chick jumped on his nose,
they might have been the best of friends, instead of deadly foes.
He tried to extricate his head, but alas! ran out of luck,
a plank came down upon his crown, and so his head got stuck.

His front was in the chicken house, his brush was in the field,
it seemed to him that this was not the way to stay concealed.
The chick meanwhile did something vile, not really meant to please,
his feathers tickled Foxie's snout, and he began to sneeze.

The first 'tishoo, turned the chick quite blue, it ripped his feathers off,
he catapulted out the door and landed in a trough,
the second sneeze was no small breeze, more like a hurricane,
the air in Foxie's lungs burst forth with all his might and main.

The chicken house was first to go, collapsing round his head,
when he scrambled from the wreckage, his dinner had all fled.
Quite bruised and sore, he felt for sure, that chick had cost him dear,
he'd tear him limb from limb, he thought, if he only had him here.

As his headache cleared, what he most feared, came quickly into sight,
the Farmer with a twelve bore gun, to put the fox to flight.
Discretion is, when all is done, the better part of valour
and facing flying buckshot brought on a deathly pallor.

He fled across the stream right then, close to the speed of sound
he'd live to fight another day, but now must go to ground.
He ran 'till out of gunshot range, and then he turned about,
he glared back at the Farmer and stuck his tongue right out.

The Farmer fired a brace of shots, and singed a chestnut tree
he loaded up again to fire, but saw the Fox was free.
"I got inside your chicken house" the Fox appeared to say
"and I'll have them on my menu card, for sure another day."

AFRICA

The once proud Zulu nation has lurched into the modern era, holding fast to ritual and outward display of the warrior creed, while their appointed officials loot the nation's Treasury and abuse its womanhood.

AMA ZULU

The Ghost of Shaka Zulu
stalks the ground,
the Regiments have departed,
the Great Kraal at Ulundi.
No longer heard the Impis
beating their shields
with the blood-lusting Hlwha,
nor the battle-cry "U-Sotho"
on their myriad manly tongues
proclaiming dominance of the earth.

The War Chiefs have fled the field
their Ostrich-plumed glory
reduced to a tourist attraction,
strutting a bogus battlefield,
prancing a soap opera stage,
mouthing scripts written for them
by men of straw, in coconut ink.
All we possessed is flawed
The Tenderpreneurs 'toyi-toyi' and sing
of long laid down "Mshini Wami",
cutting swathes through old traditions,
while abusing reed-dance maidens.

The Drakensberg pound
with empty songs, ringed with lies,
the Ujenele, in fake leopard skins

lust for empty honours
falling from BEE tables,
these crumbs that do not satisfy
an ancient nation's hunger
centred in a glorious past,
as the amaZulu hear faint echoes
of the Hlwha, beating on Shaka's shield.

Ama Zulu – the Zulu Tribe
Hlwha – Short stabbing spear invented by Shaka
Mshini Wami – My machinegun
Ujene – The Generals
Tenderpreneurs – Black Entrepeneurs benefitting from the BEE Tender
process
BEE – Black Economic Empowerment.
Reed-dance maidens – Every year Zulu maidens parade bare-breasted
for the Zulu King in a ceremony called The Reed Dance. He picks one
for his next bride.

Before an African tribe is addressed by its Nkosi or King, his personal Imbongi or Praise-giver prances in full native dress in front of him, extolling the virtues of his lineage to the attendees. They sometimes carry these colourful antics into bowels of Parliament just before the President is about to speak.

IMBONGI

Bring on the toy-toying Imbongis
let the praise begin,
the raucous rhetoric
will hide our grievous sin.
The nation's treasure leaks
into Pretoria's bins
while Mbeki has his AU dreams
and Zuma is showering again.
The people will not forever
endure or forgive their chains
the neglect of infrastructure
the relentless political spin.
We are "previously lit",
not "in the dark"
improvements to health are in train
crime is being swamped by incompetence
as the Scorpions fight closure in vain.
We are content in our discomfort
to rather lose than win,
while the HIV Grim Reaper stalks,
his face in a twisted grin.

Like our complacent Harare cousins
we are eating the seed corn again,
but at least we have the comfort
of blaming the whites for our pain!!

AU – African Union
Scorpions – Special Police Investigation Unit
Imbongi – African Tribal praise-giver
Zuma – former President of South Africa who once took a shower after sex to avoid contracting AIDS!!

South Africa is populated by some of the most wonderful people on earth. Its eleven official languages reflect the amazing diversity of its people. Whether Xhosa, Zulu, Pedi, Venda, Sotho, Afrikaner, white, black or coloured, they are not well served by those who have taken power in the Rainbow Nation. An Indaba is a meeting.

INDABA

It is an African thing, this love of Indaba,
it connects us with the Ancestors
for without them, we do not proceed,
tribal agenda locked in the spiritual
no moving forward before looking back,
to the days of greatness when
at blood-soaked Isandlwana we defeated
the powerful proud IsiLungu.
The, warriors lived to hunt and fight
and wash their spears in enemy gore
while women tended babies
made mealie pap and sorghum beer.
Now equality plagues our land,
great men talk down from high places,
and say we are cherished now,
lurking jobless in our mean townships,
while they circle the globe in splendour
generating pride to place in our empty pots.

IsiLungu – The English
Insandlwana – Battle in which Zulus defeated the British Army in
1879.

I visited Mandela's cell on Robben Island, and marvelled how such a great soul could expand in such a confined space. His unworthy successors in title would do well to reflect more on the humanity of this great man.

Mandela's Cell on Robben Island

How can greatness be confined
by so small a space,
be contained in an island
of repressive thought.
How can a narrow sea channel
separate a great soul
from its needy heartland
from the graves of its ancestors
from a world craving its courage.
How can so small a space
designed to crush the spirit,
so enlarge the mind
banishing bitterness
amidst whirlwinds of abuse.
How can so small a space
nurture towering intellect
suffused with humility and love,
especially for the tormentor,
while inhumanity and hatred
insult a princely pedigree.
How can so small a space
incubate visionary futures,
for a nation riven by division
or beget the healing balm
capable of restoring pride
in a people too long nurtured
on belittling bile.

This unsettling space
is an enduring eulogy
extolling the greatness
of an unfetterable mind.

W.H. Auden spoke of Cafavy's "unique tone of voice"! A poet of another time, he is still unique in every respect. A Greek/Egyptian poet, he was born in Alexandria, but lived in Liverpool for a while, until financial constraints caused the family to return to Alexandria, Unusually, in his life he never published his poems, preferring to hand them out to friends or people in the street. He was a personal friend of E.M. Forster, and he and Arnold Toynbee and T.S. Elliott were early promoters of his work. He wrote mostly about ancient Greek culture.

CP CAFAVY

Alexandria knew no greatness
before you,
She grudged your fame at first
but you brought her forward
bruising her mind with hammer blows
of well-wrought thought.
You liberated her imperfections
bade her don new intellectual garb
cut and sewn from your great soul,
then taught her to discard those fripperies
and stand shorn of pettiness
before the great chasm
of her own unworthiness.
Alexandria knew no greatness
before you!!

Printed in Great Britain
by Amazon